IN CHAINS

THE MOMENTS WE STAND
IN CHAINS

ASHLEE BOYSON

book three

Text Copyright © 2023 Ashlee Boyson

All rights reserved. No part of this book may be reproduced in any form or by any means without permission in writing from the author.

The Moments We Stand: In Chains

Print ISBN: 978-0-9904810-6-5

Also available as an ebook

Published by The Moments We Stand

Library of Congress Control Number: 2023902968

Cover and interior design by Chelsea Jackson

CONTENTS

Preface: You Are the Miracle 7
Forward 10
Prologue: Enough..13
Chapter One: Fear with Faith 15
Chapter Two: Absolutely Not...23
Chapter Three: Face to Face 32
Chapter Four: Click 42
Chapter Five: The Broken Road to Faith..........................54
Chapter Six: Think of Me 64
Chapter Seven: All I Ever Wanted.......................................70
Chapter Eight: Choose a Side...76
Chapter Nine: Send Someone 83
Chapter Ten: Impact...89
Chapter Eleven: Victim..96
Chapter Twelve: Let It Go... 103
Chapter Thirteen: The Coat 106
Chapter Fourteen: Dateline... 109
Chapter Fifteen: Proceed to the Route........................... 112
Chapter Sixteen: Stranger... 117
Chapter Seventeen: Dr. Phil 121
Chapter Eighteen: Too Close to the Fence 126
Chapter Nineteen: A Few Hard Days Then Faith in the Plan 133
Chapter Twenty: The Strength of the Buffalo............... 140
Chapter Twenty-One: Get to Work 144

Chapter Twenty-Two: Dear Trauma 146
Chapter Twenty-Three: Look Up 149
Chapter Twenty-Four: The Same Story, Different Ending 153
Chapter Twenty-Five: Evidence 155
Chapter Twenty-Six: A New Story 161
Chapter Twenty-Seven: The End 165

PREFACE

You Are the Miracle

A WHILE BACK IN A church class we were talking about the subject of grace. At the beginning of the lesson, the teacher told us it has been said that if Christ's miracles were to all be written down, they would cover the earth many times. Throughout the class we read about all of Christ's miracles from the bible.

At the end of the lesson, I had a light bulb moment: Jesus's documented miracles were all performed in three years, and in a classroom full of people, we could read all of the stories in less than an hour.

So who were the others? Who else did Christ heal? Were all of his miracles only in those crucial years during His time on earth?

As I sat and thought about how He could possibly heal so many people in a three-year period—so many that those stories would cover the earth—I realized something I had never thought of before. Those other miracles were all of us—me and *you*.

My mind began to whirl around this concept, and I could almost see some of the silent miracles that have occurred because of His grace. Tiny moments in my life that I know didn't happen by accident. Evidence that His hand was ever present. A beacon of light to help me find the truth.

Everything that has ever happened when a miracle has occurred has been because of Him. Anytime a doctor cures a disease or a broken arm. Every time someone survives a plane crash or an auto accident or walks away from a tragedy. Every time a soul is saved, or a heart is changed, a miracle has occurred. And Christ has been there.

We see miracles every day, many of which we will probably never understand. Just like the bible, our lives are laced with reflections of His grace. But sometimes we forget it is His hand that makes it all possible. We can see the doctor and we can feel the pain leave, but the part of our healing we cannot see goes so much deeper.

Someday, maybe not in this life, I believe we will all read our own stories of grace—moments when a miracle occurred in our lives. Maybe someday in a Sunday school class, someone, somewhere, will be reading about our trials and how Christ carried us through them, working miracles along the way.

So next time a miracle surrounds you and you are tempted to think it was merely a coincidence, remember it was the Savior who made it possible.

Because of Him, we see tender mercies that help us feel that we are not alone. Because of Him, our hearts can heal, and our minds can mend. Because of Him we are each a miracle. Through every trial—whether seen by the world or felt in our hearts—He is there. We are never alone.

I had seen many miracles, but none of them would compare to the wonder that occurred in the moments after the murder trial when my eyes were opened to others in pain. I learned that there was more to life than living in the chains of victimhood. I saw that fear was keeping my hands tied. I was bound by choice. I was struggling to forgive because I thought my constraints were out of my control. Freedom wasn't about waiting for another person to break the chains I thought they held me in. My release from my bonds was not going to be from the apologies I longed to hear.

Freedom was going to be something I fought for. Walking

away from the prison where I was held captive was a journey I would do on my own, but I was never alone. Freedom was realizing that, through Christ, I had the power to set me free.

Forgiveness wasn't going to be about breaking chains. It was going to be about letting them go.

> *"To forgive is to set a prisoner free and discover that the prisoner was you."*
> Lewis B. Smedes

FORWARD

AND THERE SHE WAS. BROKEN. Used. Humiliated. Insecure. Hopeless. Sleepless. Empty. Scared of the past. Fearful for the future. Even in a house full of people, she always felt alone. A victim. In every way, her pain consumed her.

Time seemed to be frozen most days. She felt stuck in a time warp—and yet everyone else seemed to be moving on. The world passed around her quickly as she longed for one thing: *peace*.

Peace. Happiness. Hope. She always looked out over the horizon searching to find them again. Her dreams were the same as they had always been, only the goal line seemed so far away. Trauma had settled deep in her bones, and the lies that it carried were dark.

So much light surrounded her, but the pit inside constantly pulled her away from it. Every day promised a brighter day to come tomorrow, but each one closed deeper in despair. "Time heals all wounds," she would hear over and over again. But each month's ending became proof that she was broken.

She began to believe that healing was something she would only read about. That grace was a promise made to those who did everything right. She started to forget the moments of miracles along her path and longed for the day she would again be worthy to feel His love.

And so she waited. She waited every day for perfection to come and make her feel whole. Perfection. Yes, she knew if she could find a way to fix what was broken, *then* others would love her in the way she "deserved." *Then* Christ would come and make up for all that she lacked. *Then* God would send the angels of light to help her feel peace.

Perfection. It would come, and *then* she would love herself. But until that time, her battles would be lonely. Until she found her desired perfection, she would live in the prison of hate and fear.

The stories are all the same. The characters change, and the surroundings are not consistent, but one thing is for sure. Anyone who has ever been through trauma can attest to the battles that can literally knock us off our feet.

We thought the defining moment was hard, and then we are set into motion on a highway full of demons and battles we do not feel prepared to fight.

Depression, anxiety, waves of fear, trust issues, low self-esteem, broken relationships, anger, rage, lack of appetite, closet eating, binge shopping, addictions, overpowering hobbies, lack of interest in anything that used to bring joy, trouble sleeping, fears when cooking, loneliness, hopelessness, delusions, blaming, projecting, and hatred of self, to name a few, are the real battles.

The trauma was just the moment we were opened up to the lies about who we—or we assume others—believe we are or have become.

Take the girl at the beginning of this chapter. She became blinded by a fog. Those are the lies she believed. That defining moment of impact opened her up to a lot of truths—truths about her story and truths about everything that was going wrong.

But one thing they never told her about her trauma was that the beliefs she would take on about herself weren't true.

You see, trauma puts us in a state of shock, and in those critical moments we are opened up to all the dark things that surround us. We see the world as flawed—sometimes for the first time in our lives—and in those moments of feeling the darkness surround us, in come dark beliefs about ourselves, about the world, about others in our story, and even about God. Beliefs that feel so true that we spend the next few years or decades finding evidence to prove to ourselves why we still believe them.

We are set up to fail. Triggered by anything reminding us of that broken person we think we have become. Triggered back to a moment of trauma with the belief that we have a job of protecting ourselves from it ever happening again.

So we battle with fear as our weapon. We yell, and scream, and beg. We hide out in quiet rooms. We suffocate anything broken coming from within, for fear our acknowledgment of it might make it believe that it is welcome. We cope in ways we never thought possible, and shame ourselves for not being strong enough to get out.

We hate ourselves. Not because something bad happened to us, but because we are scared that those beliefs that we took on in those moments are in fact true. So we avoid anything hard and pray to God that all will be set right, deep down believing that maybe it will be our own death that frees us from this hell.

We are trapped—in our minds, in our hearts, and in our story with a dark fog consuming all we used to be and shielding us from all we once hoped we would become.

We find ourselves hoping that this trial will be our last, feeling forever stuck in a cycle of self-hatred, fear, and shame. Stuck in chains.

Little do we know, as we fall victim to being bound, victimhood isn't chains, it is just a rope we choose to hold onto. Victimhood isn't a trap. It is a choice.

PROLOGUE

Enough

AM I ENOUGH? SUCH A simple phrase, yet an overwhelming fear that can consume a life.

And it did consume a life: mine.

At this time, I still struggled to find my worth every single day. I longed every moment for the awakening I thought the murder trial would bring. I ached for hope and searched high and low for peace. I waged through deep fears that didn't show any sign of relief.

I struggled in my role as a mother, feeling inadequate at every turn. The truth of who I had decided to marry started showing up in all sorts of addictions and struggles, which only added to the stress I already had heaped upon my shoulders. In more ways than one, this new marriage was the do-over I had prayed for in my closet the night Emmett died. Little did I know that it wouldn't end the way I had seen it in my dreams where Emmett didn't die.

Day after day, a message would swirl through my head that I wasn't worthy of the love I knew I deserved, the love I continued to give. With little fight left, I could barely breathe if I had to even attempt to address the issues we were presently facing. So I just pretended. I did what I was best at: I found the positive even when it wasn't there. I stayed small, so I didn't disrupt. I avoided sharing any opinions opposing his view and I did all in my power to keep the peace.

Life with an addict who had a temper had to be better than being alone through the hell of the upcoming trial. At least that is what I told myself every time a new issue would slap me across my face.

The pain of the past was more than I could bear, and facing the upcoming trial was the one thing I knew I had to tackle before I could even acknowledge the present moment—before I could even think about looking at the shame I felt for marrying someone I hadn't realized until about six months in, was just there for money. He wanted me small, he liked me broken, and he didn't approve when I started to find my voice again.

The conflict to heal the past and avoid the chaos of the day was a prison. I struggled to eat. The fear of the trial kept me in chains. I had become a victim of a murder, and I didn't know if I was going to survive.

Some moments, time seemed to stand still. Others I couldn't keep up with how fast it seemed to fly. It was a rollercoaster of highs and lows: anticipating living real life again once the trial ended, and fearing letting go of the past once it did.

So I waited and waited, each day a battle between relief and fear. I would build up in my mind the ceremony of healing the courtroom would bring, all the while losing sight of myself and struggling to remember how to live a "normal" life.

With each day that passed, my beliefs of not being enough grew strong. The voice inside of me began shouting to the fear that I was not—and never would be—enough. And the chains that held me captive grew tighter and tighter as I began to not only believe, but live the lie that all I was was just a worthless, broken victim.

CHAPTER ONE

Fear with Faith

ONE NIGHT AFTER I TUCKED all the kids in bed, Bostyn came running out into the hall. She grabbed onto my hand and pulled me back into the twins' room. She was a little bit shaky and said, "Mom, today at school we watched a video about electricity and how if the power lines are down and you get too close to them it can kill you. Bailey and I are sort of freaking out about it, and we can't go to sleep."

I sat down on their bed and tucked them back into their covers. I wasn't sure what to say, but within seconds these words came to my mind. I said, "Girls, I don't think Heavenly Father gives us knowledge so we can fear. I believe that knowledge is given to us to keep us safe. Heavenly Father wants you to know about the dangers of power lines not so you can be in fear all night and not so you can be paralyzed in fear when an emergency happens, and a power line is down. He wants you to have this knowledge so you can have faith. Faith in yourself that if that tragedy were to come up in your life, you would know just what to do.

"I believe that Satan wants us to obtain knowledge so we can fear. He wants you to stay awake all night fearing your new knowledge. He wants you to be so worried that you don't sleep all night long, then tomorrow you are so tired that you don't enjoy any part of your day and it will be no fun at all. He wants you to panic for the rest of your life so much so that when one day you come to a fallen power line you are so scared you don't know how to use your knowledge to keep yourself safe.

"I know that this knowledge about the dangers of power lines feels new and unknown, but I think that Heavenly Father sent it to you as a tool to store in the back of your mind for safe keeping. Your new knowledge isn't to be used right now because the only use for it right now does not come from God, it is fear. God wants us to use our faith to store that message of safety so one day, if we need to bring it out, it will be our faith—not our fear—that will help us remember how to keep ourselves safe."

I have no idea where those words came from inside of me, because I don't believe they did. I believe they came from God. The power in my testimony to my daughters that night about power lines spoke a million words to my own heart. There had been so many moments in those past few years when I had taken knowledge and turned it into fear. Even in the little everyday information given to me by another person, I had developed a skill to put my fear into motion from the tiniest of "facts."

Since Emmett's death especially, I had spent days and even months thinking that a knowledge of what happened with the murder would bring me faith enough to find the peace I was seeking. Knowledge in itself is a worthy cause, but when that knowledge is coupled with fear, the aftermath can be devastating—sometimes just as powerful as the event in which you wanted to obtain more knowledge about in the first place.

The trial for me was that knowledge. I craved the facts. I needed them to live. I never stopped searching for them. And any day that I would take a break from my search, the facts would find me. It was as if we were on a hunt for each other—the facts and me—each of us just a step behind one another.

Sometimes it was as simple as a nurse in the ER, after getting stitches in Tytus' finger, pulling me to the side of the building to tell me of some facts she overheard in Rob's hospital room on the night of the murder. Other times it was a random phone call from an unknown caller giving me a tip. Information poured in constantly. But when it didn't, I searched for it. Without it, I was alone.

Every eye staring my way in the grocery store was a potential bearer of the truth that I craved. Every pretty girl was a threat to the marriage I no longer had—and worse, a trigger of fear in the marriage I was trying to build. I was like a sponge that was drying up, but nothing seemed to make things right inside. No amount of evidence called in by detectives brought me one ounce of the peace I still longed for. It added to my fear.

I wanted to know why Rob took a gun. I wanted to know what was said that night. I craved seeing the note that was written to me that sat on Rob's front seat as he shot a series of bullets into my husband. I longed to hear the emails. I desired with all my heart to know the details of the life Emmett was living while I was rocking his screaming infant in my arms.

I wanted to know why Kandi and Emmett were there that night, but mainly I wanted to know why I wasn't enough. I secretly hoped that the trial would be scattered with proof of all the evidence of why Emmett was not choosing me. That way I could piece together in my mind all that I did wrong so I could change whatever parts of me had not been good enough for him. I hoped that the trial would give me knowledge about all the parts of my life I did not know—and I hoped that knowledge would save me from ever living any of it again. As insecure as the narcissists I had fallen in love with, my insignificance was doing what a narcissist magnet does best: believing that the problem was me, and finding ways to build them up. That coping mechanism kept me stuck even further from my healing, as the cycle turned me into a woman who would drown waiting for one of them to throw me a life preserver before I would ever even see that trying to hold them up was what was suffocating me.

Side note: Insignificance is at the base of every toxic relationship. Some turn it into an excuse to make life all about themselves (AKA the narcissist), while the rest of us attract someone we can make life all about (AKA the narcissist magnet), so we don't have to face how small we feel. Toxic relationships create cycles to keep each in those roles. Any interruptions of that system can spark the fear of insignificance and can become very abusive. Anger is always a cover for a deeper emotion. The narcissist will do anything to keep you stuck in fear and being small over letting their fear of their own insignificance shine through. Vulnerability becomes something they never share, but try to get you to so they can use it against you to keep you small. If you feel like you have had relationship after relationship in this cycle please come to my website (www.themomentswestand.com). We NEED to chat. There are options beyond feeling stuck in this cycle. The answer is building your view of yourself, and finding your worth without the need of approval from the outside. It is about finding your connection to God and your own strength. Find your significance and you will find partners and relationships that can see it too.

I was broken. Each time the trial date was changed, it was like another million-pound load was placed upon my shoulders. I waited like a baby bird left alone in the nest, my mouth gaping wide open, thinking of little more than what awaited, craving the facts to piece together the broken pieces inside of me.

Me. A word we victims come to think about a lot.

One day I got a call much different than any I had received. Mediation. Rob had agreed to try to mediate the case. *Mediate*—like a no-fault divorce? You take your truck, I will take ours, and we will call it fair? I wanted to throw up, but I agreed. My desire to have the trial over outweighed my need for every nasty detail.

The days leading up to mediation were heavy. I could not wait to put a face to his mug shot. To me, he was a mythical creature—maybe like a big green hulk—that had come and destroyed my world. I wondered if he even had a heart. Maybe he would look like the tin man who could feel nothing inside.

I hallucinated almost hourly what the mediation would be like. In my mind, I pictured us ending the day in the same room, me screaming and yelling at Rob all of the things *I* had been through because of his decision. I hoped my words would be given the floor regardless of anyone's feelings. I longed to stand in front of the whole room and show them that this "victim" had a voice, to show them I still had a heartbeat.

The day of the mediation came. I awoke to an excitement I had never felt before. I was nervous, but I was even more ready to have my voice heard. I had asked my stepdad to accompany me to the courthouse since he had worked as a lawyer for many years, and I knew he could help me sort through decisions. By the time we reached the parking lot, I was shaking. The excitement to let my emotions explode was like a bomb waiting to go off. My nerves had set in in full force.

I wasn't ready to face Rob, but I could not wait.

We were shown our room. Emmett's parents were both waiting inside with the prosecuting attorneys from the Attorney General's office. I hadn't spoken to Emmett's mom in over a year. Rob was in a room down the hall with his defense team. I was torn between which was my worst enemy that day—the murderer or Emmett's mom. Things had not gone well with our relationship, and there came a point when I knew I wasn't going to be able to heal and have her in my life for a time.

We waited for what seemed like four years before the mediator came to our room. He began to speak. He said something along the lines of, "Well, I appreciate all of you being here today. We hope to come to some sort of resolve by the end of the day. I will be going back and forth between the two rooms in hope that we can come to some sort of bargain that we can mediate this case out on. Once I meet with Rob and his attorneys, I will come back in here and discuss with the victims what they are willing to settle with, and we will just go back and forth until we reach an agreement."

My heart dropped. *Isn't this the day when I am no longer just a victim? Isn't this my time to let it all out and piece together all that was broken by this man? I don't want to be a victim, I want to be me, Ashlee. Please someone see how much this has hurt for me. Someone please acknowledge that it was my husband who ended up on that cold parking lot. Someone please see that I was the one that had to take care of those five babies alone. Someone see me. Please someone ... I can't ... I can't breathe.*

    I couldn't stop it. I stood and said, "Sir, I appreciate you being here and trying to work with all of us. This case ... is probably just another day on the job for you, but it is a hard one for us. I need you to know something. We aren't just victims. I know that your job is to just listen to facts of the case and settle on words, but what about us? We are not just victims.

    "I have a picture with me of five of the little "victims" of this case. Is there a time today when you get to see that, or hear about them? They each have names and stories of how this murder affected their lives. So, though I am so grateful that you are here to listen to the facts, I just need you to know that this case is not just about facts and victims. It is about people with names, and testimonies of truths that came after the gun.

    "So please, today as you speak with Rob about the hours that lead up to that gun fire, please don't forget us and everything that has happened to each of us after it. Please don't forget that we are more than just victims in a crime movie. We are people, and this has been our real life."

    All eyes were on me—some strangers I had never met, others, family, who had become strangers. Nobody knew what to do. The room was frozen. Though I didn't get to tell my stories, it felt good to have a voice—even just for a minute.

    Rob didn't end up settling on anything that day. I didn't even get to see his face, but for once since he had pulled that trigger, I spoke as his victim. Maybe not in the way I had anticipated it would be, but that day I showed myself that I did not want to live in fear. I was not a victim. At least, I truly wanted to believe I wasn't.

    I wanted to be seen as a person, and more than anything, I didn't want to hurt. But little did I know, as I longed and begged for someone to see how it felt for me, I was stuck in exactly that: victimhood.

    You see, victims can't wait for time. They want what they feel is best for them now. They live in so much fear and believe that once they are seen then their pain won't hurt as much. But the truth is having your pain seen by someone else is not what makes it feel better inside of you.

Fear. It is like an epidemic. Once it settles in us, it feels nearly impossible to break free.

I feared more in those eighteen months that I waited to break free from the victimhood Rob's gun had imprisoned me in than I had in the rest of my entire life combined.

Fear robbed me of life. Just like Rob had robbed his victims of the life they once knew and Emmett of the breath he once took, fear stole my soul from my body every single day. *Fear* kept me in victimhood, not the postponed trial, or the lack of empathy from the people I thought I needed it from the most.

In that moment, at least for a second, I felt the pull to find a way out of the chains. I wish I could say that the feeling of empowering the woman inside stays strong, but each day of the trial presented a new angle for my fear and belief of my victimhood to find its place again.

In one way or another we have all been imprisoned by fear. It drives us to say and do things out of anger. It passively waits silently for us to allow its power to overwhelm our minds. Sometimes it comes in the dark of the night when we think about a truth we have learned or sometimes it comes in the light of the day, swirling around a truth we long to hear.

Just like I testified to my little girls that night about the power of God, I have often whispered to my own heart as I was trapped in the plaguing power of fear. *He is there. He does not want fear to destroy us. He doesn't want us to live as victims. We cannot be exempt from the power of fear, but we can turn it over to God. We can testify to our broken souls that it is through Him we can find faith.*

So on those dark nights when fear feels crushing, *pray*. Ask Christ to send His grace. Pray for reassurance that the knowledge of this world can strengthen your faith. We will not fear when we are blessed with faith—faith in God, faith in this world, faith in our future, and even more: faith in ourselves.

Faith even when the scores cannot be settled in a day of words. Faith that though we cannot control the power lines in our lives, we can stand tall wherever we are.

Faith did not carry me through the mediation day until I realized that I had no need to fear. That moment when I told a room full of people that I wanted to be seen as more than a victim, for that second, I finally did. I saw my strength for the first time, the way God had seen me all along.

I was standing. And every time I would fall in the months that followed, God did not stop sending me reasons to stand.

CHAPTER TWO

Absolutely Not

IT SEEMS THAT JUST ABOUT when you have things figured out in life, something new comes up to change it all. I have always taken pride in my creations, including the ones that were only in my mind. I like to have a plan and I look forward to crossing things off as I go.

Things have always felt comfortable when life was going according to my design. A younger version of me used to believe that happiness was defined by the fulfillment of checking things off the list I had created for my plan.

I write lists—on paper and in my head—of exactly how events will go. Just like I mapped out my ideal life story with a beginning, middle and end, even in the trials I have faced, I have envisioned an "end" for each one. For me, the murder trial was going to be that "end." I couldn't wait to check it off my list as the final chapter of the unclosed book from my past.

As life will do, my plan was changed.

It was a phone call. I answered. The man on the other line spoke. He said, "Ashlee, this is Shane Bishop. I am a producer for Dateline NBC. We have been calling a few people who are involved in the Rob Hall murder trial coming up. Keith Morrison is going to be doing the interviews, and regardless of who participates, we are planning on doing an episode on our show about everything you all went through, and we were really wondering if you would be willing to let us interview you about your part of the story. We'd like you to tell us about how this affected you and your children. We think your role would really be powerful in telling this tragedy."

My heart was pounding, and just like during most other phone calls about the past, I could feel my anxiety levels rising. However, I didn't even have to think much. I knew just what my opinions were and what I was willing to do.

I said, "You know, I appreciate the fact that you are trying to put some light on this whole story, but I am not really OK with it. I don't want anything to do with it. I would actually really appreciate it if you could just leave it alone and let us all be. I haven't even decided if I am going to be able to live through the trial, let alone tell the whole world how it all felt for me. Thank you for calling and giving me a heads up about what to 'look forward' to, but I will not be participating in any of it. Do not call me *ever again*."

It was a straight up "hell no!" and no part of me felt guilty for how blunt I had been.

He was very understanding and let me know that if I did change my mind, he was just a phone call away.

Ha ... like that would ever happen. I huffed and puffed about that phone call for days. I called church leaders and my parents, asking them for advice about what they thought I should do. Everyone shared the same opinion I did: ABSOLUTELY NOT!

So that was my decision. There was no way I was going to participate in telling the emotions I felt in the story of Emmett's death. I couldn't put my kids through that. Plus, I was the mom who had called news stations yelling at them for putting our pictures on TV in the days that followed the murder. I had shut down Facebook for months to not allow anyone in and to hide all my pain.

Why on earth would I open myself up to the country about how deep it still ran? Why would I be vulnerable in telling a humiliating story about how I wasn't enough for my husband and he got shot in a parking lot for fighting for another man's wife?

And my family—we had enough on our plates. The last thing we needed was for me to open up the wounds of the past and talk about a life we did not share. I knew that would not go well.

So I did it again. I went into hiding. I shut down my Facebook account. I zipped my lips and made a vow to myself that my "story" was not going anywhere. I even began talking about skipping the trial altogether. I decided denial was a much safer haven than reality, so that is where I stayed.

Shawn came home one day and told me he wanted to take the kids to Disneyland. It felt strange planning a trip to get away in the middle of everything, but I couldn't wait to go. We left Kaleeya and Tytus home with my sister Abbey and her husband Alex. We got on a plane one Sunday morning and didn't come home for five days.

Denial of anything real life oriented was easy there. We had a blast. I felt like my mind was clear, and it was natural to forget the mediation that took place a few weeks before that had been a bust and the upcoming trial.

In denial, I didn't picture life as the limbo state I had been living in. Yes, in the back of my mind the big hurdles were always looming. But they seemed very small from where I was standing. Disneyland was good to me—it was the happiest place on earth I could have been. For a moment I could breathe and not focus on anything but having fun.

The sad thing about Disneyland—and the mystical false reality that you can live in when you are there—is that it all disappears when you fly back home.

Dateline was still going to create a show about our past. The trial was going to come. My new husband was still battling an addiction I had recently become aware of. And I was going to have to take the stand. Yes, it may have been postponed a few more times, but eventually it was going to find me, and I could feel its power pulling me the minute the plane hit the ground.

This wasn't my life. What was I doing here? How did life come to this? The dense fog that surrounded me on that runway was stronger than any I had ever seen. The world came crashing in and the darkness of it poured into my veins. I was scared. I could not take any more.

Shawn went back to work, the kids went back to school, and I sunk deeper and deeper into despair. The trial was now only weeks away, and there had been no mention of another postponement. Now, the date I had anticipated and craved to come began to be the same one I started to hope would never come at all.

I secretly wished they would put it off again to buy me some more time. Time for what? I did not know. Possibly time to snap out of the bleak false reality that I buried myself in. Time to figure out what was real. Time to talk myself out of denial and remember how to stop living like my past was just a bad dream. Some days, more than anything, I was scared to have the trial over and have to face the pain that was playing out in my new life.

I was scared to have it over, for fear I still wouldn't remember who I was after all. If the trial came and went and I was still broken, what then? It was a bipolar dance of a desperate need for the trial to come, but a frantic fear that it would not change anything inside of me once it did.

I wasn't sure which way was up. All the strength I felt I had built to get on that stand and pour my heart out to the man who had pulled the trigger began to fade.

Days became even more dark as I struggled to find my strength, and then one day it came—like many times before—in a dream.

I was sitting at a table covered in photographs. Pictures from my past—from childhood up to that present day. Pictures of my life with Emmett and others of us now.

I just sat there staring at them, feeling the emotion of each and every one. They all had a memory. As I picked up the picture of the kids and me at Emmett's funeral, I looked up and there sitting across the table was Emmett.

I stared at him in shock. He said, "Ash, one thing is for sure, you never stopped smiling. You always found the good. No matter where you have been in your life, you have seen through the darkness—a gift not many of us know—and you have smiled."

I looked around the table. I stared at each snapshot of my life and realized he was right. I could see one thing in common in every scene: I was smiling.

Even in the picture at Emmett's funeral, I had my babies in my arms and though my mouth felt forced at the time, I was smiling. I could see as I held the picture of that day in my hand all the things I had to be thankful for—all five of them. Maybe that day I felt there was no reason to be smiling, but I had done it anyway. I looked down at another photo of our family. Another hard moment. Another smile.

Emmett began to speak again. He said, "I can't change the past for you, Ash, but you can change the future. Take our story and tell everyone exactly where I went wrong. I can't change the life I lived, but they still have the chance to change theirs. You are the only voice who can tell that story now, so do it! Don't be scared. You have smiled through a lot harder things than this. Tell them the story that no one else can. Tell them to put their family first before it is too late.

"The truth about our past will save someone—maybe even more than one. You didn't ask for this, but you have smiled anyway. Don't hide. Stop pretending it didn't happen. Be brave and be bold. The one you are supposed to save will hear you. You don't have to do this for yourself—because I know you don't want to—but I need you to do it for me and everyone else who is right where I was. Your words won't change our past, but they can change the future."

I woke up with a smile on my face. I called Shane Bishop back and committed to the interview. I didn't want to do it. It went against everything I felt to be true, but I knew that my dream was much more than that. There was a greater plan than mine.

The story of Emmett's murder was not complete without the family he left behind. The details of how he died were insignificant if he was just a cold dead body. The person Emmett knew he had to save wasn't going to be changed by hearing about a few shots of a gun. They were going to be moved by a story of a family man who stood at a crossroads and chose the wrong choice.

Emmett knew it and I knew it. Our story didn't have to be in vain. Our past—full of bad choices and broken hearts—might make a difference for someone. So I committed to do it. For that one.

Dateline was going to ask about how it felt for me, and I was going to tell them. Not because it would be easy, but because I had a promise that my words would make a difference. Our hell—our story—could change an ending for someone else.

So with all the pain I had been hiding for so long, I made a promise to not hide it anymore.

~ ~ ~

The interviews could not take place until after Rob was sentenced. So now, with just weeks until the trial would begin, I had a new goal to set in my mind for when all of this would be "over."

The trial was not going to be the end I thought it would be, but another step to a new "end" of the past. In my mind, Dateline became the final chapter to this heartbreak I had carried. Once it was over, our real life would begin again.

My plan had been changed, but I was smiling.

Sometimes we have a plan, and sometimes a greater plan has us. One thing is for sure: I didn't always smile for the plan that was created for me, but I have always seen a reason to smile despite it.

The plan I created was going to be easy, but the greater plan that has been written has *created* me.

I always saw myself as an artist, sculpting and creating beauty. As a mother, I have felt my creations were close to perfect. As a painter and photographer, I have always had a vision in my mind. But as a daughter of God, I have become a work of art.

It is in those humbling moments that you realize you don't have all the answers. It's those early mornings when you wake up to understand your stubborn view was wrong or those dark nights when you are humbled to see your vision of life was only one version of the course to your end goal, that you find your relationship with God. Those moments when your humility brings you past the pride of hanging on to your own ideals and gives your life back to the One who gave it to you in the first place. That is when you are sculpted a little more to someday become His perfect masterpiece.

I didn't choose this greater plan. It chose me. So many times I have doubted my worthiness of the missions I have been asked to go on, but I have seen great blessings on those days when I didn't ask why.

Sometimes we walk blindly in faith—a gentle tiptoe, holding our hands out to feel what is in front of us—and other days He asks us to take a blind leap in the dark with no time to see what is in front of us.

Those leaps take greater faith than any of the tiny tiptoes that preceded them, but it is in those leaps that we learn to fly.

"Absolutely not." Two words I have learned to use sparingly. It seems every time I have uttered them in my life, it has turned into a learning experience—one where I had to make way to a greater plan.

It is usually in those moments—when we think we have all the answers and have life all figured out—that God gives us a chance to grow in *His* way.

Our faith doesn't grow until it is stretched. So warm up, kids, because we came here to grow.

God is there. He absolutely does not forget us. He hears our fears, and He knows our pain. But He also sees the gifts we cannot see. He knows when our "absolutely not's" can become the very thing that sets us free.

So to everyone who has felt alone on a mission they did not choose, it is going to be scary. It is going to be dark. Some days you are going to wonder which way is up. It is going to be hard.

Not everyone is going to show up for you. Not everyone is going to love you in the ways that they promised they would. It is going to be lonely and long. There will be moments when you feel you should just give up.

You will feel small. You will see yourself as insignificant and meaningless. Your pain will sometimes feel that it is all in vain. You will grieve over the lost path you thought you would take.

There will be days when you want to stand on the top of a skyscraper and tell the world of all the hurt in your heart. Then there will be days—even years—when you want to crawl into a cave and keep it all hidden safely inside forever. Some days you may even ask why.

So when those questions come—those deep dark questions that penetrate your very soul—*Has anyone ever been where I have been? Am I alone? Are my cries just echoing inside of me?*

Absolutely not.

You are not alone. Your fears are real, your pain is heavy. But *you* are not lifting them alone. Maybe life is giving you more than you feel you can bear, but He has absolutely not left you alone to carry it yourself.

Like my little ones at Disneyland for the very first time, we may feel like we are the first to experience some of life's rides. It may seem like we are the pioneers of having faith in something we cannot see. It feels overwhelming when our boat takes us on our first ride into a dark cave. But just like the log ride at Disneyland, eventually our boat will see the sun—maybe sometimes just in fractions of a second at a time—but little by little it will be there.

So look for the light. When your journey brings you out of the tunnels and back into the sunshine, smile for that little flicker of warmth that is still lighting your path.

Find a reason to grin despite the roller coasters you are riding. Sometimes you will be disappointed. Sometimes you will wish there was more excitement. Other times you will be pushed to venture onto a ride you would have never chosen for yourself. In all the rides you take there is something to be learned and experience to be gained, but we cannot do it alone. We have to turn to something more powerful than ourselves. We have to find a hero to give us strength.

We don't have to be our own superhero. We weren't meant to save ourselves. There are many in the world pretending to have all the answers to all our tough questions, but the truth is there is only One who can truly save us.

Because of Him we can smile no matter where we are. Because of Him we can find peace when the superheroes of the world let us down.

(No offense Frozone. You are awesome.)

There are not many things in this world that are concrete—even our super(est) of superheroes. But Christ is.

We can never forget that He will absolutely not leave us alone. He has been down the waterfalls you are about to encounter. He has ridden through all the dark caves. He has seen every rapid.

He is there. He is real. And He knows right where you stand.

Make sure you are taking a stand for the right causes. Don't let your list of things you will "absolutely not" do stop you from fulfilling the mission He has written to sculpt you into the perfect masterpiece He created you to become. Take that leap. Be bold, be brave, and never forget: you are absolutely not alone.

CHAPTER THREE

Face to Face

I NEVER KNEW LIFE WAS going to be filled with so many moments. Moments of much strength have come when I have least expected them, but moments of overwhelming weakness have hit at a time when I thought I was strong. It is hard to prepare for all the moments we will face in our lives because frankly, we don't always know what is even just seconds away.

There are some moments in life we face with a backup squad. We call our moms when we need parenting advice; we ask our dads to help us fix a broken down car. So many of our obstacles are easily tackled with someone else on our team—another set of hands to ease our burdens, a voice to urge us on.

Then there are those moments that we have to face head on all alone. Giving birth—yes someone can stand by your side and tell you when to breathe, or even beg someone else to come and give you drugs, but there is not a way to give any of that responsibility to any other party. Professional exams—you can study your heart out with other people, but when it comes down to the day of the big test, everything is up to you and only you.

In my younger years, I had not seen many of these "I have to face it head on all by myself" type of experiences. I have always had a team to lean on and others to divvy out the burdens placed upon me. I did not know what it was like to be placed in front of an obstacle I had to fight alone until I was face-to-face with my past.

~ ~ ~

The trial date was set and just days away. Jury selection morning was finally here. I decided to take my kids to school on the way, so I knew I was going to be a little late but it was not like it mattered. No one even knew I had decided to attend.

I had butterflies in my stomach. I was nervous contemplating seeing the faces of the people who were going to be sitting through the trial, listening to all the facts of the case. I was curious what they would look like and who they would be.

I wondered what they would think as they sat in their seats when it was my turn to take the stand. I wondered what they would believe. I wanted to see for myself so I knew exactly what to expect.

I got to the courthouse and parked my car in the giant garage. I made a mental note which level my car was on and slowly made my way to the elevator. I stared at my feet as I walked.

In the elevator the thought crossed my mind to just go back to my car and drive home, but when its doors opened, I walked out onto the sidewalk. I looked up. There it was: the courthouse where I would be spending the month hearing about how Emmett was killed.

Thoughts whirled through my mind with every step that I took. *What are you doing here? What is it that you are looking for? What if Kandi is in there? Then what is your plan?*

Like many times before, my mind went through all the possible worst-case scenarios that could go wrong in that courtroom full of potential jurors. I skimmed through all the reasons why I should go get back in my nice warm car, but I kept walking.

Once I passed through security in the courthouse, I reached another elevator. It carried me up a few flights. It finally reached the right floor. I walked down the long hall and stopped in my tracks as I reached the door. I knew that the judge and all the jury duty nominees would be sitting inside. I stood there a few minutes, trying to talk myself into turning the handle.

The butterflies were in full force. I knew the minute I turned that handle and opened the door that the past was going to be real again. I knew that I would have to take a seat, and that would mean I was ready to embrace the fact that the trial was going to start. I could see my pulse in my shaky hand as it reached for the lever.

Stop ... I am not ready. If you do this, you can't undo it. Once you sit on those seats—once that judge sees your face—you are committed to hearing the truth. What if it hurts more than you can bear? If you walk in that room right now, you can't hide from it anymore. You will hear the facts, you will see the pictures, and it will all be real. Not just real—it will be blaring in your face for Heaven knows how long this trial will last.

Last call to walk away, Ashlee. If you do this, you are doing all of it. You are coming to every minute so you can put together the broken facts and heal your mind of this hell. If you walk in that door, you will not run away. Turn that handle. This is it. Maybe you are not brave enough to do this, but are you brave enough to walk away and never know?

I didn't have it in me to walk away. I needed those facts to the puzzle that still had missing pieces in my mind. I slowly turned the knob and opened the door. There were still 100 people on the panel. The room was overflowing with strange eyes—all of them on me. The bailiff grabbed my arm and led me quietly to an open seat.

As I walked to my seat, a few people realized they knew me. The judge instantly asked them to leave. I put my purse on the ground and stared at my feet for a few seconds, still trying to understand my need to be there. I offered a silent prayer that I would be able to find whatever peace I was there seeking that day. I didn't know why I had come, but I had a secret hope that it wouldn't take me too long to figure it out.

I picked at my fingernails for a few seconds, still trying to talk myself into looking around at the strangers who surrounded me. I listened to a few different people answer the questions being asked of them by the judge. My heart dropped every time they said the word gun.

I grabbed my phone out of my purse and stared at the clock. It had only been a few minutes, but I already was getting the urge to leave. I took a few deep breaths and reassured myself that I had the strength to do hard things. I put my phone back in my purse, determined to be present in that courtroom.

I finally looked up ... into the eyes of Robert Hall.

My whole entire body froze. Including the butterflies in my stomach. Shivers went down my spine. First of all, I had absolutely no idea he was going to be there, and second, he was not just in the room. We were sitting face to face.

They had seated me—with nothing between us but a half wall barrier—a few feet directly in front of him. The room went silent around me. All I could hear was fear pushing blood around every inch of my body. I felt like I was being suffocated by the lump in my throat.

Similar to my run in with Kandi at the restaurant, my body went into fight or flight mode. In that second, everything inside told me to run—to get as far away from that man as possible. Then a wave of fight would spark my emotions, even greater than my need to run away. I wanted to start yelling and screaming; I wanted to cry and hit him. I wanted to tell him the stories that I had lived because of his choice. I wanted to show him how he hurt me, and even more, how he had destroyed my children.

My anger shook through every limb as I stared into the eyes of a killer—the man who *willingly* pointed a loaded gun at my husband, who pulled the trigger on my dreams—the man who shot a bullet into my family.

Rob—the mug shot I had screamed and yelled at many nights alone in my room—had a body? He had eyes? He was a real person? Somewhere in my mind I had imagined him as a fire-breathing dragon, or a vampire with sharp fangs.

To me, he was supposed to be a mythical creature out of a horror film—one that had no emotion and no feeling. *He was just a man?*

After a year and half of dreaming about the moment I would see him, it all came to this?

I couldn't ask him any questions? I couldn't speak to him? I still didn't know what his voice sounded like or if he had a favorite food. I knew nothing about this man. How could a normal looking person—one I didn't even know—have so much power over me?

For nineteen months I had begged to be given this opportunity—to meet the man with the gun. My requests never got approved. I had a vision of what it would look like finally being face-to-face with Robert Hall, but I always pictured it going much differently.

I wanted a minute of freedom to ask and tell it all. I wanted unlimited time to pour out the pain that was still stuck in my heart. I wanted to hear him tell me the story only he knew.

It wasn't fair that I hadn't been able to see his face long before that day when hundreds of people surrounded me, ensuring my silence. And maybe that was the plan all along.

"Victims" can't have freedom of speech, for fear their words will sway the jury. I had learned in many meetings before this day that I had to be a fly on the wall. Any emotion could be warrant for a "mistrial" granted to the defense. If the jury were to see how the facts of the case affected me, the trial could be a mistrial, and we would have to start all over with a new jury who knew nothing of our pain.

I didn't know Rob was going to be at jury selection, but I knew the rules. I swallowed my emotions and choked the tears that were building up inside of me like a volcano waiting to burst.

He would not look me in the eye, but all I could do was stare. I hardly took my eyes off of him the entire day. He fidgeted back and forth in his seat, but he never once looked at me.

I listened to everyone's voices, but I didn't hear a word. In my mind I was still rehearsing all the words that Rob Hall was going to hear some day—the heartache he had caused. The stories of the lives his decision had affected.

I found it ironic I decided to go alone that day, because that is exactly how I felt. All alone.

I guess I could have taken a friend with me, but it wouldn't have mattered. There aren't many moments when you are stuck in victimhood that you can feel them near you anyway.

A hundred people surrounded me, but I had never felt so alone in my entire life. Nobody was holding my hand and telling me what to feel. Not one person in that room knew my name or had felt my pain. Not even Rob knew that my heart was about to shatter. Then again maybe he did and he didn't care anyway.

I had walked into that courtroom prepared to begin to piece together the facts of a murder in hopes that it would piece together the broken pieces of my heart, but I was not prepared to stare into the face of the man who had caused it all.

I stared into his soul. I tried to find the story he kept buried deep inside. The one only he knew. The missing part of my story, the one where a gun was taken from a hoodie pocket and aimed at a man's head and heart. The part of the story that took away Emmett's breath. The part of my story that left me a widow at the age of 28 with five babies to raise all by myself.

This man that was seated only a few feet in front of my view—he did this to me. Because of his anger, I had been through hell. Because of his choices, my world had been turned upside down. And in that moment, I truly believed that because of him, I no longer had the choice to be happy—truly happy.

My eyes burned as I continued to choke back tears, and I did everything in my power not to blink. I didn't want to miss a second. I didn't want to look away, for fear he had that gun in his jumpsuit. Even more, I didn't want to look away for fear his eyes would tell a story the minute I did. I didn't want to look away because I secretly prayed he would see me and that he might try to understand how hard it had been for me.

When you are trying to stare into a man's soul, the only place to look is into his eyes. He wasn't looking back, but I could see them. His eyes were sad. He looked much older than his mug shot—like the year and a half he had waited for this day was even longer for him than it had been for me.

I wasn't sure if I should throw a stone at him or go and give him a hug. My heart hurt not only for the pain he had caused me and my children, but for the pain I could see in his eyes. Anxiety waved through my body as I tried to figure out if I hated—or pitied—the man that now sat in front of me.

I didn't know why, but for the first time I saw the parts of me I had lost. I saw myself as the little girl who walked around the playground looking for people who were alone; the younger me who found the lost puppy at the park and walked around door to door for hours to make sure he made it safely home.

I could feel empathy—the kind that my daughters had shown—for a few seconds. I finally felt for myself a moment of relief from the hate of victimhood.

Once the jury panel was selected and we were dismissed, I all but ran to my car. I slammed the door behind me just in time for the emotion of the day to come pouring out. I sobbed the whole twenty-five minute drive home.

I wept for the years I lost with the family I had created. I poured my heart out and all the pain I had been holding inside came tumbling out. I yelled at Rob for the gun he had used. I cursed his name for the choice he had made, but for the first time, I mourned for the pain he had caused in himself.

I stepped into his shoes for a second and I felt the deep pain he had heaped upon his own shoulders. I sobbed for his family, and the never-ending torment they must all have faced at one time or another because of the decisions of the three in our story. This story had more victims than just me—and they were all in pain. Some were victims of choices out of their control, but Rob was a victim of his own demise.

I learned a lot that day. Not so much about life or my faith, but about pain. Some pains we have to face head on. Some come because of a choice that we made. And others are placed upon us by the sins of someone else.

Rob would never tell me the stories I longed to hear, but being face to face with him gave me strength to start to let it all go. I could see his cracking soul, and I knew I wasn't the only one broken from this story. He would have to pay for his own sins, but I was going to find a way so

I no longer had to.

Forgiveness. I think I felt a glimpse of what that could mean in my life. I wasn't going to get the scream session I had longed for. I probably wasn't ever going to hear him say he was sorry, and maybe he really didn't care about how it felt for me.

For that moment, I didn't care. He killed Emmett, and he was going to go to jail, but for a few moments I saw that that wasn't going to be what healed my heart. Peace wasn't going to come by the years Rob spent in jail.

Just like Rob was that day, my heart was in chains. But someday, I knew I was going to be able to set it free.

That moment when you think you are face to face with your enemy, you feel alone. You want to run away for fear you will be hurt again. You want to scream and cry, in hopes of letting that person know all the pain you have carried because of them. You want them to hurt exactly how you have hurt.

In that moment when you realize you have let the pain define who you have become, that this enemy holds all power over you, that they have come to own you—that moment is hate.

I was comfortable with hate. I knew it well. It was powerful and up to this point, it more often than not won! In some ways it kept me alive. In others, it stopped me from living.

It wasn't until I stared into the face of my worst enemy that I realized he was just a man. It wasn't him that held the power over me. It was my own hate for everything I had come to blame him for.

The moment you are face to face with a past that has broken you may be the same moment you come face to face with the knowledge of how to set yourself free.

That moment when you realize *you* are the prisoner—not the man in chains—that is the time when you want to plead to your Father for true forgiveness.

For the first time since Rob pointed a gun and shattered the night, I felt true hope—and not the kind of hope that could only come after the ending of a trial. I felt reassured that everything would one day be made right. I knew at that moment that no matter how the trial ended, I was going to be standing.

There are not going to be many moments in our lives when we have the opportunity to stare at our pain face to face, but our struggles are real. Even the ones you cannot see are sometimes unbearable. Many people struggle with depression; some are plagued with disease. Some people have been abused, neglected, or forgotten.

We are all facing some sort of trial. Not everyone will get to sit in a courtroom through a murder trial to try to put together the broken pieces of the past, but we all at one time or another will have to face them head on. If you have spent the last nineteen months or the last nineteen years trying to run from the past, *stop*.

Running from the past doesn't change anything today. It only dilutes the happiness of tomorrow.

Now is our time to set the past free. The past was long ago—even if it was just yesterday. It doesn't have to follow you around anymore. You can start fresh today, and you have a Savior who can show you the way.

Your pain may have held the power over you in your life for all this time, but you don't need it to survive. It is hard to let it go when it has been your lifeline, but once you set it free, you will see that it was suffocating you all along. Set yourself free. Pray for the peace you are walking around seeking.

Maybe you aren't standing outside of a courtroom waiting for a reason to turn the door handle, but it is waiting for you to.

Turn the handle. Step inside. If you walk away and pretend it is not there, it still isn't going to go away. *Maybe you are not brave enough to do this, but are you brave enough to walk away and never know?* It is your time. You deserve to be happy. You deserve to smile every day.

Not every day will be breathtaking, but there will be beauty in each one.

Most days we take a few steps forward or fall a few back. On the day that I was face-to-face with the man who murdered my husband,

I didn't fall back. I flew forward. I didn't read about forgiveness in a textbook or my scriptures. I felt it in my heart.

I was face-to-face with the love that Christ had blessed me with. I knew that because of Rob, I had much that was taken from me. But I also knew that because of Christ, I could be made whole again.

My happiness had nothing to do with where, what, or how Robert Hall would spend the rest of his life. My happiness had everything to do with *me*. I was face-to-face with the past, but I was finally able to see what the future could bring.

Life is going to knock us down. It is a proven fact (at least for me) that the more we try to do good, the harder Satan will try to get us to doubt and to fall. The next month of the murder trial would be just that for me.

I would get knocked down, and then I would get right back up over and over and over again, coming face to face with reality, coming face to face with my own victimhood, coming face to face with more heartache. But even greater: coming face to face with the knowledge that I was not alone.

CHAPTER FOUR

Click

I HAD PROGRAMMED MY MIND. I knew I would have to attend the murder trial in a forced, locked down, zombie mode. I prayed that I could put myself on autopilot. I hoped I could hear and see but not feel the facts of the story that had broken me. I knew I had to be that fly on the wall—the one with no emotion or passion shown. Just an everyday citizen learning about a crime.

The scary thing about allowing yourself to slip into autopilot is that it is not easy to find your way out. Other times a single moment of weakness can lead you to snapping out of it in uncontrollable ways.

Our bodies were not made to work properly on autopilot. It is a fight or flight mechanism that was never meant to be permanent. Autopilot—or as I have called it, zombie mode—is something our bodies do to keep us safe. We can see what is around us, and we can hear, but in this type of mindset we cannot feel. It is a deep dark fog.

I had unintentionally lived on autopilot for many months, but during the trial I had to put myself back in it on purpose. I knew I could not allow myself to feel, even if I wanted to, but sometimes I would begin to feel regardless of how hard I tried to fight it. The hardest part of all was when I would go home for the night and I couldn't snap out of it. I could hear my family, and I could see their sweet faces, but I could not feel anything.

~ ~ ~

It was October 2012 and the murder trial was about to begin.

The morning came. It was still dark outside when I pulled myself out of bed. My eyes burned from the tears I had cried the night before. My heart was heavy knowing I was going to be leaving the kids all day, but I knew my mom had come to pick up my slack. I was in turmoil as I tried to accept the reality that today was the day. I was anything but prepared.

I stared at myself in the mirror. My pep talk was less than loving.

Ashlee, you have to stop. This is not about how it felt for you. You have to suck it up, get over yourself and put on your game face. Stop crying. Stop feeling. There is nothing that will be said that is going to change anything. Once this is over and Dateline wraps it up, it will be done.

You will be able to put together all the pieces and then come home and start living for real. You cannot feel. You cannot wish. All you can do is listen. The past is in the past. But today it is here again. It isn't real this time—just a recap of all that it was. Put on your game face. Stop crying. Do not feel. Autopilot time. Do not feel. Everything is going to be fine ... you are going to have to be numb. See, hear, but do not feel.

I knew this day was going to be strange. I had a new life that I was trying so hard to create, but a broken past I still longed to heal. My nerves were getting the better of me, but I tried to smile despite my inevitable butterflies. I was hopeful with the reassurance I had received during jury selection. I knew this time in court would be hard, but I felt peace that my healing would come, regardless of the verdict.

My friend Brittany volunteered to drive me down so I wouldn't have to walk in alone. It was nice having a friend to talk to on the drive to the beginning of what would come to be the longest month of my life.

By the time we reached the courthouse, I was so flustered that I was shaking. I was nervous to see Rob again, but this time my thoughts were consumed more by the fact I was going to have to face Kandi. I didn't feel prepared. I wasn't ready to embrace the pain her decisions had caused me. I didn't want to look into her eyes and search her soul for her pain. I didn't want to let go of the anger I had towards her because in my mind, she didn't deserve it.

I walked into the courtroom. My eyes darted in all directions. I scanned the room to make sure I hadn't missed any hidden corners. If she was there, I didn't want any surprises like I had been given the first time seeing Rob. She was nowhere to be seen.

I took my seat on the victim's side along with Emmett's parents. His mom and I had not had many conversations since he died. We had both taken some time to piece together our own realities.

Emmett's dad looked sick, but he was there. He gave me a smile. They hadn't been married since Emmett was a baby, so I wondered how it felt for them to sit on that bench together learning about the poor choices and murder of the one person that still connected them.

As we sat silently staring into the empty room, I couldn't help but look at the bench just across the walkway from us, full of the ones who had come to support the other side. I could see what looked to be Rob's parents and sister. I could almost feel the butterflies that must have been dancing around inside each of them.

My eyes stared, fixed on them, almost in bewilderment.

How could they come to support a murderer? Could they not see the obvious ending to this trial? What hope was inside them that brought them here? Did they think he was going to be able to walk out with them at the end of the day? How could any parent watch something like this? Maybe they are in denial about their son?

My judgmental thoughts were happy to take the place of my own insecurities. My mind did all it could to keep me from feeling emotions. It was easier to sit and wonder about others' personal struggles than to be surrounded by my own.

Soon Rob was escorted into the room. He was in chains, but this time he was wearing a suit. Not a prisoner jumpsuit—a business suit. I guess it made sense he would want to look presentable, but it was weird for me to see him dressed like one of the attorneys.

Who is he pretending to be? Does he really think a suit will let anyone see past the gun he held in his hand?

I swallowed hard, trying yet again to slow down my self-righteous mind. I guess inside since I knew I was not allowed to feel my own pain, I had created an unspoken rule that everyone else's pain was fair game.

The minute Rob took his seat and the judge began to speak, my numb mind began to slip out of autopilot. I had to control it. I pinched my arm.

Ashlee, this isn't real. You are only here as an outside on-looker. Remember, nothing you see here today is going to hurt you anymore. You have to be brave. You cannot feel. You can see, but you will not feel. These are just going to be facts, pieces to your puzzle. See them, collect them, but do not feel them.

I tried with every fiber of my being to buy my own bullshit. My heart was pounding as the jury walked in and took their seats. I tried not to make eye contact with any of them. One catch of my stare, and my secret pain would be revealed.

Tears began to form. I fought the urge to wipe them, for fear someone would see. I choked back my emotions as my throat closed off. I began to think I had made a mistake. Panic. I felt claustrophobic.

I can't do it. I can't sit here like this doesn't affect me. I can't pretend everything is ok.

It took everything in my power not to scream and run out of the room.

My eyes darted around again searching for something to stare at. Rob … jury … judge … Emmett's family … Rob's family. Nothing in that room was a safe place to rest my weary eyes. Every bench held a reminder of why I was there and a reason for my heart to feel.

I wished so badly I had the kids sitting by my side—a neutral safe haven to turn to for strength. I wished I could grab their tiny hands and try to calm my beating heart. My mind darted back and forth, in and out of the past and present, trying to wrap around what was real. I wanted to press pause for a minute on the past and step back into my present life. I wanted to go home and be surrounded by things I was allowed to feel.

Have you seen the movie *Click*? Don't you wish sometimes you could press a fast forward button through life's really hard trials? Everything would move quickly and you wouldn't be able to feel any of the pain?

The murder trial was just like that for me, only my autopilot wasn't at a fast-forwarding speed. It was all in slow motion. Oh, and I could feel the pain, only I had to pretend I could not.

I went in that day with the knowledge that I could not let the information affect me—at least I couldn't show it if it did. I knew I had to sit back and be a silent observer—an everyday citizen with no emotion to what was being said.

The only problem was I wasn't an average citizen who had come to hear about the violence that happened in my city. I was a wife to a man who had been gunned down in a parking lot. Every word spoken affected my children and me. Every fact displayed had changed our lives. I drove to the courthouse each morning already on autopilot, knowing I was willingly walking into an emotional torture chamber.

There are many forms of brutal torture. No one should ever be physically or emotionally abused; no one should ever have to watch a loved one die. I have heard stories about torture camps decades ago, and I've read many books about lives affected by that kind of torment. But I hadn't endured any form of torture in my life. I knew nothing about a pain purposefully inflicted upon me. The torture I learned about for the month of October 2012 was a different kind of torture.

This torture was a slow-motion detailed description of not only the horrible choices my husband was making, but the details of how two bullets sunk into his heart and skull.

Slow motion details of text messages and emails.

Slow motion pictures of the crime scene that will be sketched into my mind forever.

Slow motion details of the activities of three people that night leading up to 10:00pm. Slow motion details of how Rob circled around inside of Walgreens looking for him. Slow motion details of how Rob moved his truck out of the views of the camera.

Slow motion details of how he waited in that truck for seven minutes for Emmett and Kandi to return with a letter written to me on his front seat.

Slow motion details of how Emmett and Kandi pulled up together inside his truck.

Slow motion details of each of them getting out of their cars and gathering out of the view of the camera. Three people—all going in slow motion.

Slow motion details of every possible witness that came and went. Slow motion details of the angle the bullets entered him.

Slow motion details of how and where the blood splattered all over his truck and the ground.

Slow motion details of Emmett taking his last breath.

Slow motion details of every person within the sound of the gun—witnesses trying to remember if they heard a bang bang ... bang or a bang ... bang bang.

Slow motion details of every emergency person who walked onto the scene and every detective that investigated that night. Every angle and every fact that played into the murder. Three people standing at three different crossroads all coming together in one big bang.

A slow-motion explosion of bad choices and broken hearts ending a life.

Slow motion details of how two shots of a gun changed our lives forever.

A slow-motion torture I could not talk myself into walking away from.

Click. Click. Click.

I spent a month with a lump in my throat and a new kind of pain in my heart. I don't remember taking a breath in those days I spent in that courtroom. My eyes burned and my hands shook as I soaked in the pieces to the broken puzzle from our story day after day after day, every one with a new topic, a different expert explaining what they had spent nineteen months researching and analyzing.

Just like the day I spent in jury selection with my eyes fixed on Rob, I studied people's souls. I watched each movement the attorneys made. I stared into the eyes of every witness, barely able to look away.

I studied Rob and the interactions he had with his crew of defense. I eyed each witness as they came and went. I watched as Kandi pranced onto the stage and held her hand to the square. I watched Rob's family hear the same facts I did day after day after day.

I sometimes wondered if anyone else had pushed the same button I had—the one where you were put into some sort of trance resembling no emotion—but you were really dying inside.

Each day brought different knowledge—a new challenge in forgiveness of the three people whose crossroads collided that night. Every day was like someone had pushed the reset button on my remote—like the hope I had received in the past vanished into thin air. I always pictured my forgiveness road to be an uphill climb. I thought for sure that each step I took would be supported by the next step.

That month I learned that hope and empathy are very fluid. The more I heard about the bad decisions made that night, the more anger I felt towards all of them. The more anger I felt towards the three of them, the more I fought the urge to hate myself and question my worth.

Every word spoken about the affair pierced me like a knife—a blatant attack on my worthiness of being enough as a wife. Every fact proven about the gun reopened the wounds it had caused in my own heart. Every word Kandi said on that stand beckoned me to hate.

Every ounce of self-worth I had tried to find for a year and a half was lost as I lived it all again. The battle of hope and despair became a cycle I ran over and over and over each day. The search for empathy for each of their circumstances seized from my heart as I tried to force myself to not feel my own pain.

I learned a lot about the power of the mind as I purposefully pretended to be on autopilot and not feel, but felt every word. The more I didn't allow myself to feel, the less empathy I felt for them. And the less empathy that filled my soul, the more I fell back into my own victimhood.

A trial that I knew would not change anything from the past became an emotional internal battle of darkness and light. The temptation to hate had never been stronger. The battle to conceal my pain was overwhelming. The hours my body went home to try to sleep, my mind did not follow. The trance took over my body. Autopilot became me.

Shawn and I didn't talk much that month, some days hardly at all. He struggled with the energy I was putting into my past, and I just longed to have his support in closing that chapter of my pain. I saw many meals brought in, I received many hugs, but that month, I did not feel the love that was all around me, and I didn't notice the love that was withheld. I didn't know how to feel.

The learning experiences and opportunities for growth in our lives are not going to be concrete—they will be fluid. For every step we take into the light, there may be nine steps backwards trying to take us back into the darkness. Each day we will go in a different direction. Some days we will jump forward, others we will fall back.

Forgiveness, hope, charity, and empathy—all virtues we are trying to perfect—will flow in this same manner. Perfect mastering of any virtue will not come in this life. They will constantly be at battle with the opposition.

Our hearts may be full of empathy and love for a foe one day, and the next day we may again remember the pain they have caused. Some days we may fail in our battle to perfect our virtues, but we can start again the next. I learned a lot about this cycle of virtuous autopilot—the dance of despair and defeat being replaced with feelings of peace and hope.

I began to see that, for me, forgiveness and hope were not strictly an uphill climb, but a mountainous obstacle. And some days I did not win. Some moments I hit valleys; others I saw stars. Some moments I could see myself, and others all I could see was defeat.

We each hold inside us a power of self—who we perceive ourselves to be. During and even before the trial, I allowed just about anyone to determine my vision of myself. I did not know I could be the keeper of this power.

Some days when I learned different facts about the case, I willingly handed over my sense of self to the perpetrator of the crime. When they spoke about the affair, I didn't just listen to the facts. I internalized them and focused on what I did wrong. I had done little in the way of healing, and was still the same girl, who felt insignificant, as the girl who married a man who would end up cheating on her.

I shifted my power of self over to Emmett or Kandi. (Because they did this, I must be this.) When I learned a fact about Rob's actions, I internalized his decisions and shifted my power of self over to him.

This is the pinnacle of victimhood—the moments where your need for someone else to see your pain is proven unobtainable and you can't understand how you will ever live without it.

I allowed the facts to bring me to many of my own crossroads where I stood waiting for their approval that I was enough.

I listened every day for one of them to change the story. I secretly waited to hear the part when I was enough for any of them. I longed to hear Kandi say she was sorry or for Rob to stand up and cry for the pain he had caused me. I yearned to have Emmett walk in and tell me this didn't all happen because I was not enough for him. I would have even settled for the judge or an attorney or someone on the jury to acknowledge that I existed.

But guess what? Nobody did.

The battle to hate had little to do with anyone in that room or with Emmett. The difference between a good day and a bad day in court had little to do with the facts that were displayed and everything to do with the power of self I could see.

When the facts were presented, I had two opportunities—two different outcomes. One was to hold my power in my mind and allow myself to feel the effect of that decision but not allow my power to be given to that person. The other opportunity, I often allowed. When a fact was presented, I gave away the power of my sense of self, and imaginarily handed it to the person who caused the pain, longing for them to make it right. Longing for them to do what I couldn't even do for myself: see me.

And that is what made the difference between a dark or light day. The information was the same, but the way I allowed it to affect me was drastically different. Maybe Kandi was a slut, Emmett was a jackass, and Rob was a freaking idiot, but their actions were not mine to own. They would have to own their roles in the story instead of owning me.

Their bad decisions could only break me if I gave them my power and if I waited around for them to fix it. Regardless of who I was—or wasn't—those three had made their own choices, and the days I could remember that, I stood tall.

The click of that gun was powerful. Those horrible decisions, made by three people, were impactful in my life. They had changed the course of the journey I thought I would live, but they didn't break me. The only way I could be broken was if I chose to let the world destroy me—if I gave away my power to anyone but myself and God.

The world is going to try to break us. Trials are never going to end. Even when the murder trial was over, its power has never ceased to try to destroy who I viewed myself to be. The truth is, the world is never going to want us to see ourselves because the minute we do, we hold in our minds the power to be everything we were created to be.

It is not the trials in life that define who we will become—it is our reactions to them.

The days I walked into that courtroom in darkness and despair, I felt it run through me. I saw and heard with a broken heart. I hated and I despised. I was numb to anything uplifting me, and I was on an emotional journey of heartache.

But those days I walked into that courtroom willing to hear, see, and not feel the pain, but feel the spirit, those were the days I was given the miracles I needed to remember who I was.

I was not a broken widow who was going to be plowed out of her own life. I was a strong daughter of God who was being given a new way to view myself, regardless of what others saw in me or failed to see.

The past has been cracked, the pain has been deep, but I am not broken.

Because of Him, even I—the widow of a man who was gunned down in a Walgreens parking lot for stepping out on the promises he had made to me to protect me, and adore me, and hold true to our marriage—could have a life filled with dreams. I could find more reasons to smile, and see myself for who I really am.

Life is going to be a roller coaster of dark days and light days. But I can promise you this: if we pray for the ability to see ourselves as God sees us, even in the moments when we feel broken and weak, let me rephrase that—especially in the moments when we feel broken and weak—we will be blessed with a different view.

We will be given the ability to see our own strength and the gifts we have been given. We will be able to view ourselves as an eternal being and not just a temporary body. We will be able to find our ability to one day be made whole from anything in our past that has shaken us.

Some days autopilot may take the reins so you can stay safe, but don't give anyone else your power. See and hear, but only *feel* the truth.

Sometimes truths are hard to feel. Sometimes facing the truths that cracked you breaks you all over again, but it is truth that puts together the broken puzzle pieces of the past, and that sets you free from the dark roads you have walked. And it is the truth that brings you to the knowledge that you are enough.

Don't let others destroy you. Be you. Find strength in your story, even the parts that want to take your power away and leave you with nothing left.

Even if the jury of life is sitting in front of you staring and you are wondering if there is anything left for them to see, God still sees it all. He feels the silent tears you are crying inside. He hears the gentle whispers your heart is pleading.

Maybe you feel alone from where you are standing, but He is not far away. In those moments that darkness has surrounded you, and you wonder if everyone has forgotten who you are, pray that you can remember, even if no one else does.

Sometimes the greatest miracle of all is waiting around for someone to see your worth, but finding it for yourself instead.

God's not dead. He lives. He is waiting for each one of us to remember Him, to find hope not only in our stories, but in His creations. He sent His Son to die for us so that we could one day live again. So we could make it through the trials and the days our bodies go into autopilot.

He knew it would be hard. He knew there would be no remote to click fast forward through the darkness and the pain, so He allowed His perfect Son to die to atone for the world.

Grace. It is the power that is inside each one of us. Because of Him, the trials we endure pretending we do not feel the pain will strengthen the view we have of ourselves. The power that lies in each one of us is greater than anyone else can see. It is a hope that only we can find in the stories only we can live.

Believe in Him. Believe in his plan, and never stop believing in the one person he gave you to be your greatest cheerleader: *you*.

No one else has been where you have been. The pilot of your destiny is you. Truth is, you are His greatest creation of all. And when you can see that, you will know that He is not very far away.

CHAPTER FIVE

The Broken Road to Faith

WHY DOES IT ALWAYS FEEL as though my faith has to be challenged for it to grow? Is there no other way? Can't there be an easy route? Or is there one and nobody has told me about it and I keep taking the long way? Sometimes I wanted to scream, "Didn't we already cover this one?"

At that point in my healing I had started asking, *Why is it that the same lessons seem to repeat themselves for me?* Obviously, I still had room to grow in all of the areas of my faith, but sometimes I failed to see why the same challenges had come up over and over. Why couldn't I learn all I needed the first time around?

The perpetual lessons of faith had been the catapult for my growth, but the pattern of their reoccurrence had also become a trigger for my fear.

If the lessons of the past have been what have taught me to rely on my faith in God, and if there has always been a pattern of these lessons coming up again to make sure I fully comprehended their magnitude, I feared one day I would have to face every pain of the past all over again. If every obstacle I had ever crossed seemed to be accompanied by a follow up lesson, I had begun to question, what on earth do I have to look forward to?

This had become one of my greatest battles since Emmett was

killed: to let the past be in the past, and to have faith in the future.

Fear of the past and fear of the future had come to define my thoughts and challenge my peace as they had battled each other. My pain of the past had caused me to hold onto fear in an effort to protect myself from obtaining any more of it.

Some days had been a unique rollercoaster of holding on and letting go and surrounding myself in a wall of fear, always hypothetically prepared for the next storm to hit. But somehow this way of living had been the one thing keeping me from living at all.

I remember a day at the murder trial when I had become so numb it felt I was no longer hearing about Emmett. I felt like I was genuinely learning about facts from a movie. Specialists were being marched on and off the stand. I saw many hold up their hands and swear to tell the truth. I don't even recall what types of experts they each were. I just remember they came and went more rapidly than normal that day.

The afternoon was progressing well, and I hadn't even had to pinch my arm to keep from crying all morning. I felt strong. I felt reassured that I was capable of making it through without causing a mistrial by my own overreactions to the facts.

A new witness was brought to the stand. The prosecution went through all of their questions smoothly. As the prosecuting attorney took her seat, the judge invited the defense to take a turn questioning the expert. The defense attorney rustled around in a bag before standing to face the witness. As he arose from his seat, he pulled from his bag an oversized picture of Emmett—one I had purposefully never seen before.

Every detail I had tried to avoid for so long flashed boldly in my face. I could see Emmett's bluish-purple shirt—I had washed it just the day before he died. I could see his dark thick hair—I had cut it every month since the day we met. I could see his hand—with no sign of a wedding ring. I could see his face, and his skin and his big eyes.

All the parts of him I loved were captured inside that picture, but all over the body that was lying on the ground was blood. He looked broken, empty, and haunting, because he was dead. For the first time since he was killed, I had a view of what I had not seen.

Instantly my mind whirled through every detail of the moments after his death. To the viewing where I tried to see through the makeup that covered his wounds and find the man who I had shared my dreams with, to the funeral where thousands looked to me to find peace, to the burial where my children screamed at me to let them open the box and say goodbye.

I could not breathe. Before my screams hit the air I ran into the hall. My panic attack was stronger than any I had ever felt. The hallway was long, and each step I took felt full of all the pain I had been bottling inside. Finally, I reached a door I could hide behind. I pulled it open to find stairs leading up and down. With no knowledge of where either of them would lead me, I threw myself onto the window's ledge and hugged my knees tight to my chest.

I sobbed like I have never sobbed before.

It was real. It was all real. These facts about bullets and blood—they were not just stories and words and percentages. They were real. Emmett was the man in that picture. He was the man we had been talking about for days on end. He was the man who had written all those emails, and made all those phone calls, and slept with another man's wife. He was the man who angry bullets had caused to fall to the ground. He left me here. It wasn't a movie. This was all real. Emmett was really dead—and he died fighting for her.

My chest pounded as the sobs finally found their freedom from the prison they had been hiding in. My head throbbed as my tears burned holes in my cheeks.

Soon, the victim witness coordinator found my hiding place. As she walked through the door, my emotions finally came out in words.

I sobbed, "Do they not know he was a real person? Do they forget who sits behind them every day? Do they not care that this changed our world? Does anyone want to know how this all felt for me or for the kids? He was a person. He was ours. He was their dad. They act like this is all just a movie we are critiquing, but those bullets … they killed a man.

"That angry gun was fired at a father, and they silenced a husband. I won't ever get to hear 'I am sorry.' Do they not understand that? He was a man, not just a bloody body on the ground. Are they going to show a picture of him when he was alive? All we talk about is the body. Do they even know he was real? These aren't just facts. This isn't just a story. That gun changed our lives. This is all real. Emmett is dead because of that gun, and that gun was fired because of that man."

My heart gaped open wide and the wounds inside were exposed for the first time in a long time. The tears continued to fall, and the sobs did not cease. Each breath I drew in was like a desperate plea for someone to care I was alive, or at least remember that Emmett once was. Each sob that forced itself into that empty stairway, a lonely song that felt as if no one would ever really hear. Each tear that fell, a hope for someone to remember the life that was taken that brought us all there.

It felt freeing to release all the emotions that had been eating me alive, and to have an ear to hear them. She didn't say much; she just let me get it all out. Soon my body calmed down, and my breathing became more consistent. Then she began to speak.

I don't remember everything we talked about in that stairway, but I do remember she sat by me for some time. She told me about her baby boy, just a few months younger than Tytus. She told me about his Halloween costume and their holiday plans.

She told me about her memories of the times we had spent together, and our conversations on my couch the night Emmett died. I remembered her being pregnant, but not much of what we had said to each other. It was strange to reflect upon that raw moment of finding out all the truths.

What a blessing it was to know she was sitting with me all those months ago, and she was right by my side again, symbolically holding my hand through another broken moment. My heart was filled with gratitude that I had been blessed with a friend who had, in a small way, been where I had been.

I have always said there is a glimmer of hope every day. This day, during a long murder trial full of silent despair, my tender mercy came in the form of an unexpected friend. In a time when I felt so alone and like no one cared how all of those facts had felt for me, she did.

I needed a friend—and God had sent me one.

The hard thing about glimmers of hope is the moment when they fade away. That night the hope had faded into fear—fear of the future, fear of loss, fear of love, fear of everything I had seen and felt coming true again. I lay in bed unable to separate the pain of the past from the fear that raged inside of me about our future. I didn't look at my family or touch them for fear I would love them and lose them.

So many of the nights during the trial went just like that. The new details to add to my remembrance of the past were like adding fire to the open flame of the fears that burned in my heart. Some days it was hard to find hope or remember any of the tender mercies I had been blessed to see.

Most of the time if hope had shown its head during the day, by the end of the night my mind had twisted it into fear, taking those facts and putting them into hypothetical scenarios for my future.

In life, sometimes it is hard to see the light at the end of the tunnel. I promise I understand! Every day seems to present itself with a new angle to challenge our faith and cause our hope to cease.

I started to accept the fact that I would never arrive because whenever I felt like I was almost there, I was thrown a new curve ball or blindsided with a flash of the past, igniting my fears at the drop of a hat.

I remember one day sitting in my therapist's office. I was stuck in the pain of my story and fearing the future with a new husband that wouldn't stop buying new cars and taking money out of the kids' college funds.

I kept spewing out all the fears that had consumed me that week. I told him about all the possible scenarios that played out in my mind in my weakest moments of fear about what was to come. I hashed over the past and cried about my paranoia of how it was replaying, and if I could just save him, it wouldn't end the same.

The therapist finally slowed me down and said, "Ashlee, I want you to look around this room and name twenty things you see."

I looked at him dumbfounded, questioning in my mind, *now how the hell is this going to help me figure out my struggles today, Doc?* Reluctantly I began. I said, "Well, I see a clock. I see a telephone. I see a box of Kleenex. I see a bookshelf ..." And so on and so on.

When I was done, I waited silently for the moral of the story. It finally came. He said, "Ashlee, what were you thinking about when you were telling me your list?"

I replied, "Well ... nothing really. I was just trying to find my twenty things. I was just trying to focus on what you asked me to do."

He said, "Exactly. In that moment you were focused on what is going on right here and now. You were not worried about the past, and you were not fearing the future, because you were focused on what was right in front of you at this moment."

A light bulb finally turned on.

He said, "Ashlee, your story has been hard. The past has tried to destroy you in ways not many of us will ever understand, but you have to let it free, because the more you hold on to it and fear that it is duplicating itself, the more you fear moving forward.

"You fear your fate because of the past, and because of the turmoil you are in, but if you don't start living in the present, you are not going to have a future. It doesn't matter if Shawn is an addict, sometimes verbally abusive, and you and him don't work out. I don't know what the future of that marriage looks like, and frankly that isn't what you can control. I am talking about you. Your future, your joy, and your healing. You have to start focusing on healing yourself, and the things you can control."

Today? Was that really the answer to my fear? Living in the moment? It all made sense, and it was so clear how true that statement was. My fear of the past was destroying my view of the future. In that moment I prayed with all my heart that I could take this do-over God seemed to be handing me and help us fight through it together.

In that moment, in my mind, Shawn's struggles were a gift—the do-over to everything that was taken from me in my marriage to Emmett. I was going to be able to stand with him, and we were going to come out stronger on the other side.

We were going to be everything I had prayed for Emmett and I to be. The couple that makes it through the hard. We were going to fight together. I wasn't going to fail. I was going to focus on the positive, see the good in him, help him in his addictions, set healthy boundaries, forgive the pain, and move forward. We would make it in the ways Emmett and I didn't get the chance to.

The truth? I knew deep down we wouldn't make it, and my counselor was trying to help me find my strength because I am pretty sure he knew we wouldn't either.

It got so bad that I only stayed because I couldn't let myself fail, I couldn't "take away another father figure" from my children, and I couldn't leave Jordyn. The shame of realizing you manifested and attracted the same type of narcissist who really doesn't care about you felt like a darker hell than living with him.

"Failing" was not an option at that point. I wanted the comeback story, the do-over I had pleaded for. So eventually I didn't even stay because I could keep focusing on loving him, I stayed because I couldn't face failure.

So I lived in fear. Not just about the past, but about the lies and secrets that were pulling me down every day. Eventually they became what pushed me to find me for myself.

In time, it was the put downs and the rage that made me realize I had to find my worth all on my own. Eventually it was the fight I was doing on my own for us to come out stronger on the other side that helped me remember my truth.

Fear is toxic, even more poisonous than pain.

Our pain is what we try to protect with our fear, but ultimately, we just cause more of it. We become control freaks, not because we want to make everyone do things our way, but because we don't ever want to lose the things we love or are trying so hard to love. Letting go of this fear is really just accepting the fact we do not own the control.

Life is so hard. It is scary, the unknown. It's frightening to think about all the possible scenarios that might play out tomorrow. *What if someone I love dies? What if I lose at love? What if someone hurts me? What if the answer to my prayers is a different kind of hard I am not ready to face?*

I didn't know when I was a young girl that so much pain was going to come my way. I had fears like any young child, but the actual fears that tried to destroy me were created by actual pain I had felt in my life. So I guess you can say they are mine to own—they were creations of my own mind. But one thing I finally realized: if I created those fears, I guess I am the only one who can overcome them.

Every single day holds a reminder of the pain, but in my experience, dwelling on protecting myself from it only causes intense fear. And no night spent in it has destroyed the pain. It has consistently created more.

We cannot control tomorrow, no matter how much we worry about it today. With that knowledge, I am fighting hard to live in the moment. When I am present, I do not feel the pain of the past, or the fear of the future. And that is a freedom worth fighting for!

Take a moment wherever you are to look past the pain, to push away the fear, and to see the little glimmers of hope that are right in front of you. Maybe it is an unexpected friend who wipes your tears when a picture of the past flashes in your face, trying to slap you off the track of hope you have been clinging to.

It's going to be different for each of us each day. Maybe today it is a warm hug from the autistic son who rarely shows affection. Maybe it is a phone call from your mother you haven't spoken to in years, or maybe it is merely the sun shining on your broken heart.

I can't promise every moment of every day will bring you joy, in fact, a lot of them are going to be dang hard. But I have a testimony of living in the moment, seeing the beauty in the beast, and searching for a glimmer of light in the dark.

So, when you get blindsided by the pain of the past, don't let your fear cause you to forget to see the friend who is wiping your tears, or the hand that is trying to hold yours through your lonely sobs in the night.

Avoiding pain is more than controlling the future—it is living each day to its fullest. When we are living in today, we are not consumed by tomorrow or stuck in yesterday. I believe it is then that we get to heal from the pain of the past and we are blessed with faith for whatever is to come.

Look around the room. Name twenty things you see.

Look in the mirror, past the pain and the broken heart and into the perfect soul inside yourself. Deep down inside each of us is a spirit rejoicing just to be alive. That spirit has a perfect knowledge of why we are here.

We each have a mission—a unique plan designed to refine us so that one day we can become as perfect as the spirit that urges us to seek for hope in ourselves. We each have our own personal broken pathway to our faith.

Fear is the lack of hope. The only way to fight fear is to find hope—to have faith for things we cannot always see and live today for a future we don't always know.

God is near. In fact, for all the things we do not understand, He will one day help us see how it was all part of His greater plan. Turn to Christ when the road gets dark and the fog is too hard to make it through. His hand is never far from yours. Reach to Him, asking for help with the lack of faith that keeps you from overcoming your fears.

Through His grace, all things are made whole. With His love, even the broken roads that brought you here can be made your pathway home.

Whatever hand you have been given, don't let it stop you from playing the game. Live for today and let go of the yesterdays that are holding you back from smiling tomorrow.

Maybe your road to faith has not been paved in gold and your pathway to heaven has been hard—mine too! We are all part of that same club—our very own earthly fight club.

All the roads that lead to faith are broken. The difference between the outcomes has more to do with what we do with our fear and how we develop our faith.

Pain is real, and fears run deep, but faith is greater than them all. So that moment when fear is planning your fate, pray for the truth to know how to see yourself as you really are.

May this moment be enough to remind us just how near we are to Him. May every broken road bring us hope for things we cannot see, and faith to live each day for a future we cannot know. Not all yesterdays are worth living for, so live today like you almost forgot just how broken it has been. This moment—right here and now— is the one worth fighting for.

The broken road to your faith is perfectly imperfect, and so are you.

CHAPTER SIX

Think of Me

EVERY HUMAN ON THE EARTH longs to be remembered. In the small mundane day-to-day tasks or the big projects of life, we don't ever want to feel forgotten.

We like to be acknowledged for the things that we do and noticed for the sacrifices we make. We like to be seen when we do something right and still loved through our mistakes. We want to be remembered when we aren't around and protected even when we are. It is a basic human desire to be remembered by others.

When you are the victim, it isn't just a human desire. It is your very lifeline.

As victims, we wait for someone to see us and long to be remembered in a way we never knew could feel so pathetic. We feel unwanted, unimportant, and small. We feel forgotten.

One thing I have learned is that some days we will be forgotten. And no matter how much we long to be remembered, sometimes it is not enough.

I knew all along the day would come, and eventually it did.

There she was—the only witness—standing on the stand raising her hand promising to tell the truth. The only person who saw the gun fire. The only one who actually knew exactly what happened that night.

I could not take my eyes off her. I had to hear it all for myself. I forced my mind to listen to every word in hopes of finding answers, or at least finding a way to stop needing them.

Why? How? When? A murder, an affair: the two things that had taken over my thoughts and had filled my soul with doubts for which I constantly was seeking answers.

As the first words came out of her mouth my heart yearned for her to look toward me and say how sorry she was for all I had gone through. I kept waiting and waiting like a pathetic junior high girl waiting for someone to ask her to dance. I just knew she had to have been thinking of all the pain the kids and I had suffered because of that night. She just had to understand my need for any of the three of them to offer me some sort of an apology.

Every few questions I leaned closer, hoping to catch the words I somehow was waiting to hear.

Soon, the two of them glanced longingly toward each other and whispered, "I love you." My heart began to pound out of my chest. A hatred I have never felt before raged in anger and resentment.

How dare they pretend that everything was OK between them? How dare they make a mockery of the fact that I would never have that chance? How dare they pretend that they could overlook the bad decisions they each had made when Emmett was killed because of his?

A black hole engulfed me as I let my hatred kindle in my heart. Ultimately it was because of them that Emmett was not there to look across the room from me and tell me the "I am sorry" I still longed for.

Did no one think of me? Did anyone remember that I had a voice— that I was even alive?

That night, did they honestly think they were the only three people in the world? Did not one of them remember I was sitting at home with no answers, trying to figure out how to be enough? And all the while a collision of bad choices were being made to prove my fear right.

My mind reeled with every question and every doubt it had stored inside.

Each word she spoke drilled and drilled into me a message I had feared: *You were not enough. You were not enough for that gun. You were not enough for her. You were not enough for Emmett. You were not even enough for anyone to walk away. You are worthless, and no one is thinking of you. Not then, not now, and maybe never.*

My heart yearned for someone to think of me—even just for a moment. I needed someone to remember the pain I had suffered or the burdens I had come to bear. Engulfed in the victimhood of my circumstances, I sat longing for relief.

I looked around the room—no one was watching me. After all the times I had wished everyone would stop staring my way, for the first time I wished someone could see me. Anyone. I wished someone would come take the stand with proof that anyone knew or cared who I was.

I wished Kandi would look out into the crowd and tell me she knew it had been hard for me. I wished Rob would stand up and say how sorry he was, and that as he was reminding Emmett to go home to his family, he himself should have thought of us before reaching into his hoodie pocket for his gun.

I felt so alone I wanted to crawl into a hole. I felt so small I could almost feel my self-esteem melting into the floor.

The hard thing about waiting for someone else to help with your healing is the feeling of brokenness that comes when they fail to meet your silent expectations. And we victims know about these silent expectations because in our minds, everyone else should be on board with our healing.

Ironically, Kandi did the opposite. Every answer she gave was different from the one she had reported the night of the shooting. Her lies didn't just make me feel forgotten. They made the truth ache to be remembered.

She was on the stand for two separate days. I could see in my mind every story she told. Her in his arms as I laid in a hospital bed with a new baby. Him in her arms taking his last breath.

I tried to picture where I was in every story. Home. Cleaning up the kitchen. Making his favorite food. Taking care of his babies. Crying in my closet for the answer to my fears. Memories of how I was forgotten became more proof of my worthlessness.

I studied her, trying to find what she had that I didn't. Looking for answers that could help me understand why he had chosen to go that night and fight for her.

I searched for something to justify how it was all worth it—why she had been worth fighting for when I hadn't. All I could find was more pain. My soul longed to find the proof of why I hadn't been enough.

I walked to my car that second day like a beaten puppy. Picked on. Alone. Forgotten. I felt like the only person in the world who had ever felt so battered. The loneliest victim I had ever seen.

On the drive toward home, I felt deflated. Not because of the facts I heard for the thousandth time, but because of the words I did not hear.

I hated her. I hated that she couldn't see me, that she could still love her husband after all he did in front of her. I hated that she held Emmett in her arms as he died. I hated that she had been enough for him to protect—and that it meant I wasn't.

I hated that I couldn't stand looking at myself in the mirror, and because of the three of them, I didn't know if I ever would. I hated that I was me—the loser who had not been remembered.

After some time of driving silent in my anger I flipped on my phone and let my music play.

Soon the playlist turned over and a familiar song came on. It was a song I had taught my little sister Ali's young women class at our church a few years back. Tears began to fall as I felt each word sink into my heart with a little glimmer of light.

Do you wonder if he knows who you are?
Do you wonder if he knows the secret pleadings of your heart
He has numbered every sand of the sea
And he longs for you to know that he believes in you.
Can you feel the quiet power from above
Can you feel his strength surround you
when your own is not enough

*He has blessed you with his spirit from on high
And he longs for you to know what lives inside of you
Oh, be true
Daughter of a king
The Father's royalty
Heir to His divinity
He's calling your name
To come and take your place before His throne
He has always known
What He created you to be
A daughter of a king*

*You hold the promises of all eternity
Rise to claim the noble birthright you were sent here to receive
He has loved you since you lived with Him before
Let him lead you to the gifts He has in store for you
Oh, be true
Daughters of a king
Our Father's royalty
Heirs to His divinity
He's calling our names
To come and take our place before His throne
He has always known
What He created us to be:
Daughters of a king.*

"Daughter of a King" by Jenny Phillips
(words used with permission from Jenny Phillips)

In that moment I felt it—that perfect love. Not for her or Emmett or Rob, but for *me*.

I was surrounded by the love of One much greater than the three I had been waiting for. I remembered the truth of the promise that was made to me long before I even came to this earth: I was enough for Him.

In that very moment my heart was overwhelmed with the love of God, and I could almost no longer remember the hate that had entrapped me for two days.

Truth will always win, for it is in truth that we find someone who *will* think of us. We find the true healing we seek when we are able to reach to the One who will always remember us.

Just like I had many times before, I walked into my house, not surrounded by the hate I had for myself and for those who had forgotten me, but filled with the love of the One who had remembered.

We are always going to be reminded that we are not enough. We are easy to forget when something seemingly greater comes along.

But I promise you this: Someone is thinking of you. He not only thinks of you when you feel alone—He remembers you when you really are forgotten.

CHAPTER SEVEN

All I Ever Wanted

IT CAME. THE DAY I had dreaded for almost two years—my turn to take the stand.

I don't remember how I got there that day. Besides Rob, I don't remember who was sitting in the courtroom watching me. All I remember was gasping for air. When they called my name, I had to physically peel myself off my bench and force my body to walk up.

Each step literally felt like I was carrying a thousand-pound weight—the weight of my reality. Once those words left my mouth, the stories I told were real. All those months pretending like it didn't happen would be over.

As soon as I found my seat—after holding my hand to the square and promising to tell the whole truth and nothing but the truth—I was asked to turn around and identify who was in the picture being projected behind me.

The first thought that went through my mind was that this was a trap—they had blown up a picture of Emmett's body lying on the cold ground and wanted to show the jury how that image affected me. The fight or flight mechanism began to sound sirens in my mind.

I swallowed the lump in my throat and felt brave as I glanced toward the picture. There it was, as tall as the ceiling: one of my favorite pictures ever taken of Emmett and me. Almost in a sigh of relief that it was a picture of his smile and not his blood, my heart started pounding.

My mind slammed me back to the very second that picture had been taken. Emmett had passed the bar. I was barely pregnant with Tytus. Life as I knew it was close to perfect. We were getting ready to go on a date with his mom and stepdad in celebration of his success as a new attorney.

I remember thinking as I kissed my kids goodbye and drove to the restaurant that night, *This is all I ever wanted.*

Tears began to fall as I slammed my mind back into reality—the one where I was sitting on the stand, not as Emmett's wife, but as a victim in a murder trial. I could not hold it together. I don't remember what they asked me as I tried to get a hold of my emotions. I do remember with each question asked I fought more and more to even find my voice.

The lump only grew larger as the questions rolled on.

Like a robot I answered every one, but inside I was beginning another round of grieving the life that had been taken from me.

I wanted to scream it from every corner of that courtroom. I wanted to yell and share my pain with anyone who could hear my voice. I wanted to tell Rob everything his gun had done to *me*. I wanted to let my hurt show.

But all I was asked were facts—where and when, times and places. The only real emotion that was involved were the ones I was being forced to hide. Rob didn't look up. Nobody asked how it felt, and in my mind, I was sure nobody even cared.

When my time on the stand was over, I felt like that puppy again—the one that had just gotten beaten up. All the stories of our pain were on the verge of seeping through my skin.

Somehow, I had built up the day in my mind—the day when I would take the stand—as a day of ultimate healing. I had envisioned telling the courtroom everything I had ever felt, and in my vision they all cried with me—they all felt for me.

Like a deflated balloon, I walked back to my seat. Months of rehearsing silently felt like wasted time.

You see, when you are the victim, the only people who can fix you—in your mind—are the people who broke you in the first place.

By the time I reached my car that afternoon my deflation had turned into fierce anger. The minute my door slammed shut, my heart gaped open and my empty car heard all the emotions that had not had a voice that day.

It started out as a gentle plea I sang to myself. Quietly I began to speak under my breath, "Nobody cares about you, Ashlee. They don't care that you have spent almost two years as a broken shell of yourself. They don't care that every time you go to cook a meal for your family, you can hardly breathe thinking of the past.

"Nobody cares that you have spent countless hours wiping tears in the night and praying on floors that bad guys won't come in with a gun. Rob didn't care about you when he put that gun in his pocket. Kandi didn't think of you as she was held in his arms. Nobody gives a shit that you thought you were living your dreams."

By this time, I was pulling out of the courthouse parking lot and onto the open roads. The angry under-my-breath voice gave way to shouts of pain.

I screamed at the top of my lungs. Some of the screams were at the gun. Some were at the man. A few were even aimed at Kandi, but most of my anger was at the man in the picture who had abandoned me that night. I spoke louder than I ever had before to a man who wasn't there.

"Emmett, that was all I ever wanted. That girl in that picture—she adored you. She had set goals in her life, and she had watched them fall before her feet. And she deserved them because she fought every day to make the right choices.

"She spent her entire life protecting herself so she could be worthy of such blessings. She went to college so she could be smart enough to teach her family. She woke up every morning to be the best gosh damn mother and wife—and she had everything she ever wanted. WHY WASN'T THAT ENOUGH FOR YOU? WHY?

"She spent her life living to make you happy. She would have gone to the ends of the earth to make you smile. Why weren't you at home fighting for *her*? Why wasn't *she* the one worth dying for?

"All I ever wanted was to be normal, to have a normal life. I gave you everything. That girl in that picture thought she had it all. She truly believed that anyone cared. But the truth is, nobody does. Rob didn't care about me as he planned your fate. Kandi didn't give a hell who I was as she pranced around in your arms.

"And YOU. If I was enough for you, you wouldn't have left me that night. You wouldn't have shared something special with *her*, but even more than that, you wouldn't have made me believe I had all I ever wanted. All I ever wanted was you, and our family, and to be enough for you. The only dream I had was to be all you ever wanted—to be the girl worth dying for."

I haven't had many grand dreams in my life. I never thought I would run for mayor or be the first woman president. I never wanted to invent something or fly to the moon. Honestly, I never set many goals outside of my home because I had everything I had ever wanted right in my arms. I never hoped to have a huge career or even work at all. Maybe I was naive, but my dream was to be an amazing wife. I always hoped to be an incredible mother—I never wanted to miss a second.

It was hard to embrace the blatant belief that was now mine: I was not enough. I truly believed that day that I had lost the only goals I had worked my life to achieve. If I wasn't even enough for the man I had given my life to, I had failed at everything.

I wasn't enough for Rob. He knew my name, even wrote me a letter. I wasn't enough for Kandi—she had sent me presents and cards when Tytus was born; she had shaken my hand and said my name. I wasn't even enough for Emmett. He didn't die proving to the world how amazing his wife was. He didn't even die fighting for me. He was shot fighting for someone else.

There hadn't yet been a day in my life—and there hasn't been any since—when that lie was drilled any harder into my mind. On that drive home from the courthouse, I was consumed with what appeared to be my inadequacy of being—every dream I had ever lost felt like evidence of my apparent failure.

At an all-time low, I could not see one ounce of the worth of my soul. I could barely see the worth of my existence. I looked upon my past as if the lies that had broken me defined who I would become.

As I pulled off my exit, I knew I had to pull it together. The dark fog had grown so thick around me I could barely spark the desire, but I knew I had to snap out of the fears that were driving me home. I uttered a tender prayer.

As I spoke, I burst into tears, this time with the real emotions that had driven my anger. I whispered, "Dear Heavenly Father … I feel so alone. I wasn't enough. Nobody cares what I went through. Nobody knows how I feel. I am alone … I can't feel anything through this pain. I am suffocating. I am … I can't, I can't breath … and nobody cares. I wasn't enough for him … I am not enough for them. I wasn't enough for anyone. All I ever wanted was for him to adore me. I just wanted to … I had it, I had all I ever wanted … why wasn't I enough for *him*? Why wasn't my plan enough for *You*?"

I continued to drive, but for once in silence. My car pulled into the driveway and I turned off the ignition and shut the garage door behind me. I sat quietly in the empty garage. I sighed a few times, hoping to catch my breath. My head fell onto my chair. I pushed the seat back until I could no longer see out the window. The garage light shut off and soon I found myself in the darkness.

Hot tears streamed down onto my neck. Everything inside me hurt. The overwhelming feeling of inadequacy steamed out of each tear that trailed down my face.

I uttered one last plea, "Why wasn't I enough for *You*?"

The most overwhelming feeling of love and peace flooded into my pitch-black car. In my mind a few words echoed inside of me, "Ashlee, maybe you were not enough for any of them, but you are enough for Me. I have not left you alone, and I will stand by you forever."

A glimmer in the dark.

Grace isn't living only in the light, living our perfect plan, checking off the boxes of all we ever wanted coming true. Grace is the little glimmer of His love while we figure out how to step out of the dark. The dark will come. It is up to us if we fight our way back into the light.

Life is going to be filled with thousands of moments, and in most of them, we will have to do a lot of standing on our own, but we are never alone.

Maybe we aren't enough for anyone else, and maybe we have lost all we ever wanted, but that doesn't take away our worth. We were created to be strong, but even when we aren't, we are enough for Him.

My tears have burned many streams down my face. A gun shattered many holes in my family. I did not know how to see myself when so many others had reinforced my fear of not being enough. But that day, even when reality reminded me I wasn't the one worth dying for, I was blessed to remember that someone already had.

Maybe nobody will ever tell you any of the reasons you are worth living for. Maybe nobody will ever die fighting for you. But Jesus Christ did.

He is the reason we are enough—because for all the days we find ourselves standing alone, we will look back and see He was with us all along. If all we ever want is for someone to believe we are worth dying for, the truth is, He believes it, and *He* has died for us.

CHAPTER EIGHT

Choose a Side

ON THE DAY THE JURY went to Walgreens to see the crime scene all mapped out, they first allowed us, as victims, time to walk through with the detectives and ask questions.

I remember getting out of my car shaking because I was so nervous. I wanted to burst into tears. It was daytime, but the chill in the October air was not much different than it would have been that cold March night.

There was tape blocking off the parking lot. That sight alone sent chills down my spine. There were markers for everything—where the gun was found, where the cars were parked, any spot blood had fallen, where Rob was found … and where Emmett had died.

My mind fell back to the day the kids and I had spent in the parking lot, trying to figure out where he had taken his last breath. Now I knew. A desire I had months before all the sudden slipped away as I forced myself to learn more truths.

While I walked around looking at facts and listening to evidence, my mind played the scenario over and over again, each time watching him fall to the ground where markers now showed the outline of exactly where he landed.

All of the sudden I looked up and spotted a man with a camera hiding on the other side of the parking lot snapping pictures of us. I wanted to run across the stalls and punch him in the face.

What on earth was he doing there? What part of this pain we were battling was worth sneaking pictures of us as we worked our way through it? I felt violated and broken.

My panic and the thoughts I had been fighting all morning about facing these hard truths soon gave way to an all too well known humiliation: I had no idea where those pictures were going to end up. That vulnerable feeling caused me to leave that parking lot feeling even more alone than I had in the fog of darkness that had surrounded me examining the murder scene.

I couldn't even grieve and heal without someone watching?

My bitterness nagged at me for the rest of the day, and soon we all found ourselves back in the courtroom. Hate festered in my heart as I stared at the back of Rob's head, this time with a perfect knowledge of exactly where and how he executed his plan.

I saw him as a beast those days—a monster. Each day that passed, my desire to find forgiveness gave way to my need for justice to be served.

The Sunday before Rob was to be sentenced, I sat quietly in the back of a Sunday school room. A question was posed to the class. The teacher asked, "What is the difference between justice and mercy?"

I don't remember who the teacher was or anything else said that day, but I will never forget that question.

Mercy. Justice. What did those two look like standing side by side? How could they—if possible—be used together? I spent a lot of that afternoon challenging my belief in their definition and how to apply them to myself. What was justice supposed to look like if I was viewing the world as Christ would? What mercy was I supposed to be seeking?

A few days later the trial came to an end, and we were asked to leave the courtroom so the jury could take the facts and determine a verdict.

A few friends of mine had come to take me to lunch. We decided to make our way down to the just-opened café on the bottom floor of the courthouse. I was almost annoyed that after spending a month in that building today was the day they opened, but as I pushed through the doors, the smell of good food replaced the annoyance of all the days before when I had to search all over downtown for my lunch.

I wasn't sure I had an appetite, but my stomach had a different opinion—I was starving. We ordered our food and made our way to the table. I threw my purse on my chair and headed over to fill up my drink.

As I reached for the ice lever, I realized I was standing right next to Rob's sister. Anxiously, I started to panic. My first thought was to just go sit back down and give her some space to fill up her drink, but as I turned to leave, I reached for her arm.

I got a little choked up as I spoke, "I … um … I don't know if we are supposed to talk, or what the rules are on all of this, but I … I just want you to know how sorry I am for all you guys have had to go through. This can't be easy for anyone. And I want you to know … I have prayed for your family, and I can't imagine how this has felt on your side of the room."

She stared at me. I had no idea if I had just offended her or if I was totally out of line. I started to turn to leave. With a quiver in her voice, she leaned in and said, "We have thought about you guys as well, and I can't imagine what you have been through. I have thought about your kids … and you."

And there it was. Someone *had* thought about me. Someone really did care how all of this had felt for us. For the first time I realized that the man that pulled the trigger was a brother. He had a mom and a sister and a family who loved him. Not because he was perfect or because they didn't hear the facts of the choices he made. Just as I had said I would have stayed by Emmett's side as he worked through his struggles, Rob had a family willing to do the same for him.

Unconditional love is sitting through a month-long murder trial on the other side of the room—the one where people stare from their seats and send hate from tear-stung eyes—for someone you still have faith in. It's being willing to sit behind him and let him know that no matter what choices he made and what facts prove his mistakes, you'll still stay, because you love him.

All of the sudden, realizing there was another side to that

courtroom, my view of the verdict began to get foggy.

Waiting for a jury to decide the fate of a man is an experience that is hard to explain. It is a nerve-racking situation full of fears, emotions, and internal battles. My heart felt torn as I watched his family and thought about the children who called him father.

My twins' words echoed in my mind whenever I battled the need for revenge, "But Mom, what about his kids? If he is in jail, then all of us will lose our dads." The empathy my children had shown that day when Rob was to go back to jail pulled at my heart and beckoned me to find forgiveness yet again.

The dance I now was swaying to was one of the need for justice and the hope to find mercy inside myself. Forgiveness didn't seem possible if I was filled with a desire for a sentence to put him behind bars. My mind was filled with the emotions of who I needed to be and what I was to hope for.

The clock seemed to slow down as I waited in a small room hidden away from the world. Friends would stop by and bring me snacks and a few laughs, but the pit in my stomach was not fed by anything they brought.

My left eye literally started to twitch just hours after we were sent to wait for the jury. Every few minutes it would start to spasm and there was no way to stop it. It felt like the outside of my body was about to have a breakdown to match the inside chaos I was facing all alone.

The time we would have to wait was unknown and even the days could be unnumbered, but while the jury was in session, I wouldn't leave the building.

For almost two years I thought the pinnacle of my healing would be the day of the trial when Rob was sentenced. Boy was I wrong.

I had been put up in a tiny room where no one would know where I was. I got word later than everyone else that the jury was ready, and I frantically ran to the courtroom. As I walked in the back door, the judge was already announcing the verdict.

For the first time, I stood in the center of the room and had a perfect view of both sides. That moment I had long awaited became like nothing I could have ever prepared for.

I looked around the room and it felt as though everything was in slow motion. I looked at his mother and sister and watched them as they heard the judge announce, "Second degree murder—30 years in prison."

I was filled with turmoil as my body told me to celebrate justice and my heart told me to mourn with those who would now be mourning.

I have never lost a child to death. I have never had to hear that my son's actions would take him away from me. But that day my heart hurt for two mothers: Emmett's mother and Rob's—one praying for justice and the other pleading for mercy.

Why does life have to be so hard? Why can't we all just win? Why do we have to choose stupid choices and react to our fears? Why do we have to feel hate? Why do we have to choose a side?

Justice and mercy. Mercy tells us we must forgive, whereas justice tells us those who do wrong must be accountable for their actions. Sometimes when these two collide inside us, it is hard to choose a side.

Maybe justice was served when a jury sentenced Rob with second degree murder and put him behind bars. Maybe that was supposed to heal parts of the broken pieces inside of me. It didn't. But what it did do was remind me of the mercy Christ has for all of us.

He is that sister, that mother, that literal Brother sitting behind us, even when all the facts point to our sentence. He is there. He is always going to have our back, even when we don't always feel we deserve it.

His mercy and His grace make it possible for Him to unconditionally sit on the forbidden side of the courtroom just to show us He still cares.

His grace not only can but *will* heal those broken parts of us that don't get put together in the ways we think they will, especially after a month-long murder trial waiting for the justice of the world to make us feel complete.

His grace will be the mercy that helps us forgive and move forward, even when we think all we have left to do is fall. His grace is enough for you. His grace is enough for us all.

Sometimes we may have to choose a side, but He will never leave us alone. Some days we may sit in a courtroom all by ourselves, or in an isolated room waiting for a jury to decide the fate of a man who has wronged us, but I can promise you one thing: there is a side we must choose, because if we don't, we will fall.

The line between the darkness of this world and His light grows even more clear as we understand that mercy is what heals our wounds—love and hope for a greater plan. Justice may bring an earthly calm, but it is mercy that will bring peace that can last forever.

For all the things we do not know, we will be blessed to one day understand. I am starting to have faith in this truth. I don't understand all of the hard things that we face in our lives, but I do comprehend that these struggles will strengthen us to be stronger than we ever knew.

We cannot choose what happens to us, but we can decide where it leads us.

I would have never chosen the side I have had to sit on—the victim's row. I have spent many days paralyzed in a world of unknowns. The unseen fear that has racked my soul has sometimes been more than I can bear. The battles of darkness that have surrounded my young family have been wars I never knew we would have to face, but we never faced them alone.

We are strong. We are still standing.

As I sat years later at my first *A Reason to Stand* conference and listened to many stories much different than mine, I realized something about the human race. We get to choose a side. We get to choose if we will stand. Life is going to continually give us reasons to find excuses of why it is easier to fall.

We will constantly be at a crossroad, and we will have to decide which side we will choose. Standing is a personal choice we must make each day regardless of where we are. Some of the strongest people I have met—the ones who stand the tallest—are quadriplegics who will spend their life in a wheelchair.

Life isn't about how tall we measure up, it is about how strong we can become when all we are surrounded by is ugly and dark.

The dark days are going to come. The one thing we know for sure is that we control nothing. We will hurt and we will lose. We can wait around for justice to bring us a false sense of our own power—a patch job for our pain—or we can begin to understand that mercy is what will make us whole.

Just like with Rob's sister at that café all those years ago, I don't know how this all works. I don't know if we are allowed to help each other through the hard days when we are forced to choose a side, but I hope someday we all understand the power of healing what is really broken.

For all who have ever waited around for justice to set you free, *stop*. The answer of mercy may not change the outcome of what justice will bring, but inside our hearts we can use mercy to find a way to remember that we are all children of God. We have a Heavenly Father who loves us all, no matter what side of the courtroom we are sitting on.

He will always have our backs. We are, and always will be, enough for Him no matter where we stand.

CHAPTER NINE

Send Someone

THE WEEK THE TRIAL WAS over, I remember slipping into a deep depression. All the weight of my emotions that I had pictured would be lifted still settled deep inside.

The fears that haunted me had not ceased. That miracle rooftop moment like on *Beauty and the Beast* where the light beamed through his entire being and the complete healing I had craved still had not come.

I was still hurting; I was still broken. It didn't make sense. Rob had been sentenced—shouldn't I have felt some sort of instant relief? I had hundreds of powerful moments of light. Shouldn't they be sustaining me still?

It was time to be back on my normal routine. I was walking kids to school and packing lunches. I was scrubbing toilets and folding laundry. I was doing all the normal mom things I had always done, but instead of feeling a sense of freedom from the past, I was grieving the reality that my burdens did not feel lighter.

Early one morning, I loaded my car with kids, dropped the four big kids off at school and headed to the grocery store. I dreaded being in public. As I drove, tears fell down my face and the cloud of gloom I thought had been bad steadily grew worse.

By the time we pulled up to the grocery store, I was a mess. I didn't want to be seen in public. I did not want to have another stranger walk up to me and ask how I felt about Rob's sentence. I didn't want to get out of the car.

I said a small prayer as I turned off the ignition. I whispered in my mind, "Heavenly Father, I can't kick this darkness. What is wrong with me? It is over, and I can't let it go. Today I need help. Please send someone to help me. Please send me someone who can ease this burden. I am alone. I feel so alone. I need someone to help me. Please help me feel less alone, please send me someone to ease my pain. Send me someone to help me learn how to live a normal life again—a friend—someone to help me remember how to keep going. Help me find a purpose. Please send me someone."

And in that moment, the victim witness coordinator knocked on my window. No, wait, she didn't. Absolutely nothing happened. Silence. I sat in the silence blowing up balloons for my very own pity party. I didn't hear any powerful words in my mind or feel any sort of answer to my prayer.

Finally I felt angrier sitting in the silence, so I wiped my tears and stubbornly got the two kids out of the car and we headed into the store. In a fog, Kaleeya, Tytus, and I wandered the aisles without much order. They snacked on crackers and giggled with each other, all the while dropping a path of crumbs in case we could not find our way out. I quietly grabbed things off the shelf and threw them in the cart.

Soon we found ourselves in the bulk food section. I began filling bags and writing down the corresponding number on the ticket. From the corner of my eye, I saw a woman standing in the aisle and staring into her cart. I turned my head towards her. Something felt wrong.

I stared for a few seconds trying to piece together what she was doing. She didn't move her gaze from her cart. Instantly I felt this strong urge to help her. The first thought that popped into my mind was to offer to pay for her groceries. Trying hard to mind my own business, I brushed the thought aside and pushed my cart around her and headed to the other end of the store.

We made our way to the dairy section and loaded the cart with milk and eggs. The nagging feeling again came over me and ushered me to go back and offer the woman some financial assistance. I battled with my thoughts and, like I had many times, I talked to myself.

First of all, Ashlee, you have enough of your own problems to deal with. You don't need to worry about someone else's burdens. You don't even know what is wrong with her. What makes you think she isn't going to be insulted by you offering her money?

Besides, how many purchases do you need to make in the next few days for your own family? Don't embarrass this poor woman by making her feel like a beggar on the street. You are a hot mess. Just finish shopping and go home.

Again, I shrugged off the impression. But as I walked, I found my cart turning to the back of the store and again past the bulk section. She was still there, looking into her cart, and then back at the food in the bins. In a panic, I veered my cart down the baking aisle.

I was almost in tears. I silently prayed.

Heavenly Father, what the heck is going on? I see this lady standing here in this grocery store, and I am overwhelmed with this feeling that I need to help her buy food. I can't do that. I won't.

First of all, she is going to think I am judging her. She is going to be embarrassed. I am going to make her feel like a charity case. She looks like a very hard working woman—I don't want to insult her.

Plus, Kaleeya needs a new winter coat. Tytus needs new shoes. Bailey and Bostyn need piano books, and Jordyn and Teage keep asking for new hats. We have plenty of things in our own life where our money needs to go. Why would I spend it on someone else? I am overwhelmed with my own burdens and trials, plus, I can't embarrass this woman.

I am just not going to take this on today. I am going to mind my own business and go home. Besides, what do I have to offer? I have nothing left of me to give. Send her someone worthy of helping her.

I started to move my cart forward to walk away. My once clouded mind became full of a very clear plan. *Get into your wallet and give her the money.*

In humility, I stopped the cart. I was sure there was no money inside my wallet—I rarely had cash. As I opened my wallet, in a zipper I hardly ever used, I found a one hundred dollar bill.

Tears filled my eyes as I remembered where it came from. After much healing in our relationship during the mediation, Emmett's mom had sent a card with money to take the kids to a movie. I had thrown the money in my wallet but used my credit card at the theater.

I stared down at the money in my hand. *I guess Heaven had a plan for you, little bill.* I choked up as I squeezed it in my grip. I slowly pushed my cart toward the back of the store, with the money still tucked in my palm.

This money and all that I have isn't really mine anyway, is it? If this is where You need it today, then I will go.

There she was—still in the same spot she had been for the last twenty minutes during my pity party rebellion. I pushed my cart alongside hers and stopped. I grabbed her arm and she turned and looked at me.

I choked out my words. I said, "I know you have no idea who I am, and I have no idea why I am doing this. I hope I do not offend you in any way, but I just need to give you something. So from one stranger to another, this is for you."

I opened my sweaty palm to reveal the money. She looked down and burst into tears. She spoke through her sobs, "How did you know? I have been standing here for a long time, trying to figure out how to pay for all these groceries. I have $13.00 in my bank account. How did you know I needed help? I needed someone to help me. Thank you. You are an angel for me today."

She threw her arms around me and continued to thank me as we embraced. My heart was so full I could feel Heaven surrounding us. We held each other for a few more moments and sobbed together. She thanked me and again asked how I knew.

I said, "Have you ever had one of those moments where Heavenly Father asked you to do something, and you almost thought He was crazy? The last twenty minutes I have been fighting the feeling to help you. But I couldn't walk away. I do know this: His love for you was stronger than my pride. You are loved, and today I think He needed you to know that in a different way. You are not alone. He loves you."

She hugged me again and we said goodbye.

I will probably never know her name. I have no idea what her story is. But that day, when I begged Heavenly Father to send someone to help me, He did.

Maybe I was an answer to her prayer—I will never know for sure—but she was the answer to mine.

For almost two years I thought overcoming victimhood was going to be done by others helping me find my way through the fog. I was waiting for them to heal. I had been given glimmers of light showing me the path out of every dark day, but for the first time I realized, as my kids had done almost two years before with a little box of letters to "people of Japan," that victimhood ends when you realize there are other people in the world who are hurting. I hadn't yet felt the pain from across the ocean, but I got to see it in the face of someone in my own backyard.

Everyone is hurting. Some days God sends us little angels to remind us that we are not alone; other days He sends us to be the angels to help us understand the world revolves around so much more than just ourselves. While surrounded by another's pain, it is easy to forget our own for a moment.

For years everyone around us had lifted me. Finally, He let me take my turn to carry some of the load.

To anyone who has ever felt alone, you are not. He is near, I can promise you. He has heard your pleas—sometimes for a temporary need, and other times for an answer on how to live again after one of life's trials.

All of us—all of God's children—are pleading for something. That day I was pleading for Him to send me someone. But "being that someone" reminded me of His love, not only for His daughter in the grocery store who needed Him, but for me.

Be that someone. When you can't remember why life is worth living, remind someone else of all the reasons they should.

He can't always send us exactly what we think we need, but His path is exactly where we need to be.

Heaven had a plan for that little one hundred dollar bill, and your Heavenly Father has a plan for you. Maybe you have been crumbled a few times; maybe you have been lost in a dark wallet for a while, but your worth is great to Him.

He hasn't forgotten where you have been left alone. He still remembers how you have hurt as you have waited for a break from the pain. Maybe you have been used; maybe someone has told you that you were not worth much. No matter how many times you have felt like you have paid for someone else's happiness—or for someone else's pain—you are still a one hundred dollar bill.

You are as prized today as you were the day you were born. Heaven has a plan for you. Maybe He can't always send someone to pull us out of the darkness today, but He sent His Son to earth to live and to die for us. That alone is enough for us to know how great our worth must be—even our story can be made whole through Him. God didn't just send someone—He sent *the* One.

Maybe I thought I needed an angel that day, but being one brought me closer to Heaven than I had ever been. It was my first breath, a first step, to break the chains of victimhood. It wasn't just a moment into the light, but a leap out of the darkness. The gift to see, the gift to feel, and the gift to be His hands.

I walked a little lighter that day. It changed me. It was the first chink out of the chain I had been carrying. I pushed my cart out of the store a different woman than the girl that had walked in. I wasn't broken, and God wasn't going to stop showing me my worth.

Look for the moments you can be His hands. It will be healing, it will be powerful, and it will be freeing. The chains of victimhood cannot be carried away by anyone else. Team with Christ to learn how to be set free. With Him guiding you, you are the answer. He is the strength you need to become enough. He is the answer and the way you will find your worth again.

CHAPTER TEN

Impact

CHRISTMAS TIME AFTER THE TRIAL was when we were asked to write our victim impact statements.

For weeks I avoided even thinking about writing my statement. It weighed heavily on my mind, but in fear, I pretended I didn't remember its due date was looming.

Finally, after a text from a victim coordinator reminding me to get it turned in, I knew I must begin. She was right. If I didn't turn in my statement in advance, it would not be approved in time for me to be allowed to read it.

I couldn't wait to read it. I didn't want to write it, but I couldn't wait to say the words that had been eating me alive in the dark of the night. I couldn't wait to take my place on that stand and tell the stories of my pain. I couldn't wait to give voice to the impact that gun had had on my family.

I finally found a free moment and headed to the solitude of my room to begin writing.

I sat on my bed, staring at the blank computer screen. I didn't even know where to begin. I would type a few words and then erase everything one letter at a time. Thoughts whirled through my head as I stumbled over every memory of the previous year and nine months.

Some versions began with anger, others with pity. Some started out with tears, others with hate. But every version would be erased from the screen just as fast as it went up. Nothing felt right.

I offered a silent prayer, hoping I could put into words the impact that had changed my life.

Thoughts continued to run through my mind.

Gun ... Rob ... impact ...
Rob ... gun ... Emmett ... Kandi ... impact ... impact ... impact ...
Walgreens ... impact ...
Rob ... gun ... Emmett ... kids ... impact ...
Kandi ... affair ... impact ...
Emmett ... truck ... Walgreens ... gun ... impact ...
Rob ... gun ... impact ...
Widow ... alone ... kids ... baby crying ... impact ...
Detectives ... trial ... gun ... impact ...
Dark ... alone ... enough ... impact ...
Emmett ... gun ... impact...
Head ... heart ... broken ... impact ...
Murder ... gun ... impact ...
Impact ... impact ... impact ... impact ... impact....

I got stuck on the word "impact." What did it mean? I knew how I had been victimized by that man and that gun, but what impact had it had? How was my life impacted by that choice Rob made to take a gun?

I clicked on my Internet browser and searched. I wanted to understand why; I needed to know how.

At first, I wanted to know what to write about—to see if someone who had been in my shoes had any advice for me.

Nothing I typed in the browser got me anywhere. So, I just typed in one word:

I M P A C T.

I read some of the definitions out loud.

Im·pact: The action of one object coming forcibly into contact with another; the effect or influence of one person, thing, or action, on another; to have a strong effect on someone or something; affect, influence, have an effect on, make an impression on.

It was so clear. In that moment I knew exactly why I was not able to put into words the feelings of my heart. It was because I was forgetting the impacts that made me a survivor.

I was focusing so hard on all the impacts that made me a victim that I was writing my "victim statement" without my whole heart. I was writing about impacts with hate in my heart and revenge in my mind. I was forgetting everything but the fear. I was trying to put into words my pain without remembering the light that had carried me through it.

All of the sudden sentences began to form, but my thoughts were not about the impacts I had intended to write about. My tears began to flow as my words came to life on the screen.

Dear friends and family,

As I have been starting to write my victim impact statement this week ... how Rob and his gun have affected me—and my children—it has brought back a lot of memories. It has reminded me of some of the pain and hurt that have been so long ago suppressed.

Reflecting on those times has not been easy, but it has also given me the opportunity to think about the impact all of my friends and family have had on us too. I have lists of thank you notes I still need to write from the last year and nine months.

Hundreds of people who have been there for me in many different ways: endless dinners and treats, house cleaning, laundry doing, blankets sewn, girls nights, alarms installed in hours, birthdays, visits, presents, closet organizing, compulsive furniture rearranging, pictures taken, sweet emails and cards, sitting with me at the courthouse for days on end, babysitting, befriending my children, shoulders I have cried on, encouragement, and prayers, etc. Only I have not written one.

Every time I have tried, for some reason I have been scared that even thinking about any of those times would strike reality back in my face. There have been months that I have been nothing but a shell of a person and have pushed everyone away. Maybe not openly, but inside there have been days that I just wanted to be done with it all. I have pretended that if I just don't even go there that somehow it would all disappear and the pain would stop and the fear would just dissolve.

If I have ever sat with you in a crowded room and I haven't said a word to you or you have called and I have been quiet or short, it is not because I am ungrateful or don't appreciate or like you. If you have come to my home or sent a kind note and have ever felt like it went unnoticed, I want you to know you have all been silent angels to me in so many ways.

So, as I think of all the impacts on my family since that night, I am humbled to reflect upon the blessings each one of you has brought to me. Each relationship the kids and I have had, have been unique and special, and as a whole, the impact you have brought has been immeasurable.

Thank you for being a kind friend, a patient neighbor, a loving primary teacher, and all the other roles you have played in our lives. Our lives are forever changed by a gun, but have been forever enriched by the people around us who have been there to help us find strength and courage and faith enough to remember that our Heavenly Father still loves us.

He makes that clear every day by the people He has placed in our lives. I love you all so much and am truly grateful from the bottom of my heart for all that you have been for me.

Merry Christmas and I hope as this year closes, we can all strive to be a little bit more like Christ in all we do. He is the reason for this season, and He is the one thing we can always count on in our lives.

No matter where you are or what you are going through if you let Him, He will comfort you. I love you all so much. Have a very Merry Christmas!

Impact. Every moment can impact us for good or bad. Every person we meet—and the actions they choose—can and will impact our lives. The times when we fall victim to these moments, we will feel the impact more powerfully than anything we have ever felt.

I have said it a hundred times: we are all going to be victims in one way or another. But not all of these impacts will leave us as survivors.

Survivors are found when we are able to see the love that surrounds us, the impact of hope, and the impressions that are made from the earthly angels sent to lighten our load.

We have to look for the impacts that are helping us survive. We must remember that writing our impact statement at the end of a hard trial isn't just to reflect upon the impact of the pain, but it is an opportunity for us to remember all the impacts that have changed us. That is the moment we will understand *"Why?"*

So much of our lives we are going to ask *"Why?"*. So many things we will endure will not always make sense. Life is going to test us over and over again, day after day, and we will be impacted by something in each and every one.

We will impact this world for good or for bad; we will all leave our mark.

Christmas that year was a wonderful time to reflect upon how we can make a difference. Christmas is more than a celebration of the birth of our Savior. It is a time when He hopes we can reflect on the impact we can have in the lives of those around us. That Christmas, the greatest gift I received was remembering the good people that had impacted us for the better.

The impressions we leave aren't just up to chance—they are up to us. Remembering Christ in Christmas is just the first step to truly allowing the impact He left for the world to ring true in our own hearts. Remembering Him is not enough. We must strive to be like Him. We must live each day so the impact we leave on the world is that we follow in His footsteps.

To truly celebrate Christ, we cannot just remember His name. We have to remember His life and the lessons He learned and the sacrifices He made. We have to write in our hearts the impact He left for us alone.

Each drop of blood He spilt was for us as individuals … personally. As we impact the world for good with our actions, we show Him all the reasons His life impacted ours. We show gratitude for the personal sacrifices He made to not only come into this world and impact those He met, but to die for us—to impact us all.

Every choice we make—everything we do—will impact someone.

It is up to us if those impacts blast a hole in the road or if they leave hope and a pathway to follow.

Impact the world by making a difference for good. Change the lives of those around you by following the One whose impact didn't just change the world, but saved it.

Watch for those that are impacting you. Not all of them will bring light, but they will change you.

The impact of our journeys will be what everyone remembers when we die. Make an impact to remember. And remember the impacts that were made just for you.

We have all been impacted in ways we never planned—whether by a gun, abuse, disease, crimes, accidents, or another person's death. These tragedies leave holes in our lives. Our pain is real, and it runs deep in us all. We all know how to write a victim statement about our pain because we all have it inside.

Let us find a reason to see how the light of the world has impacted us. Let us look for the good in the years that have passed and remember those who have strived to impact us for the better.

There is always going to be a reason to sing the lonely lullabies of what our lives should have been, but in those notes we will find that hope drifts away.

Hope comes when we let the pain go. Hope comes as we embrace those hard trials and still see the good, looking to the future with faith that even though hard times will come again, so will the light. That is when we overcome the prison of victimhood and find beneath it the truest survivors.

Impact the world with the light of truth. The true gift that Christ wants us all to receive is the impact of His life, His sacrifices, and most importantly, His love.

No matter where you have been and no matter who you are, Christ sees the differences you are making and rejoices for the impacts you are leaving in His world.

So even if you are alone—you are not forgotten. He is the gift. Share it with the world. Impact the survivors who are searching for a way out of the victimhood that now consumes them.

We are not just victims being impacted by each other. We are survivors who are carrying our brothers back to the hope they have lost. We are impacting each other just as our Savior showed us.

To all the survivors who have carried me and my family out of the darkness: I will never forget your names. Thank you is not enough for the angels who have been sent our way.

Yes, our family has forever been changed by a gun, but the impact of the lives of those who have touched ours for good will be forever remembered in our hearts.

CHAPTER ELEVEN

Victim

IT TOOK A LONG TIME for me to get my victim impact statement out of my head.

Every version I wrote became part of my continued battle between justice and mercy. I couldn't wait to tell Rob how his choices had broken my family, and I knew I would never forgive that gun, but I wanted to forgive him.

That day I took the stand as a girl who had survived victimhood.

First, I talked to him directly about my battle to forgive him—the man whose voice I had never even heard, the man who took a gun. I talked about my struggle to find forgiveness for his wife and the choices she made, and the impossible battle to find forgiveness for a husband I would never see again.

I held up a picture, one I had taken in the weeks before Emmett died. It was a picture of all five of our kids—Tytus was just a few weeks old. They looked so adorable, and their smiles were like beams of sunshine. As I held it up, tears began to fall from my cheeks. I said, "I have had the pleasure of taking care of a few 'victims' that couldn't be here today—except they aren't just 'victims.' They are five of the most amazing children I could have ever asked for. They have been my strength and I wanted their voices to be heard today."

Then I played a video statement from each of my kids. (A few days before, in a family home evening lesson about forgiveness, I had shared with them what I was preparing to do that week. They asked if they could come with me and tell Rob how he hurt them, so instead I let them do a video of their statements.)

My twins each talked about how much his choice had hurt them and their family. Teage just cried uncontrollably and said, "I don't want to talk to Rob, I don't ever even want to hear his name ever again."

Kaleeya talked about her Doggy Doggy and how Daddy Emmett gave it to her and she takes it everywhere with her, "In spring, and spring, and summer and summer and everywhere!" Then I showed a video of the first time Tytus danced. At first he started out really slowly and uneasy, and by the end he was laughing and smiling and shaking his whole body.

Then I got the chance I had been waiting for. I got to read the statement I had been writing in my head every day for two years. I had gone over it again and again any time I was alone in the car. Its words built up inside of me every time I sat outside my son's door at night listening to his sobs, or mornings when I had to force myself out of bed.

I looked straight at Rob as I read:

Dear Judge,

My name is Ashlee. In March 2011 I was married to a man named Emmett Corrigan. We had just celebrated our 7th anniversary. We were married in Lehi, Utah, on March 6, 2004. Together we had five children: twin girls named Bostyn and Bailey who were almost six, a four-year-old son named Teage, a twenty-month-old daughter named Kaleeya, and a six-week-old son named Tytus.

We spent years together creating this family. A few of those years we were both going to Utah State University for our undergrad degrees. Next came three long years of law school in Spokane, Washington. At the finish of law school, we had just had baby number four and decided to settle in Meridian, Idaho. The opportunity to work with Jake Petersen Law helped to finalize that decision. Emmett had been in practice with Jake since the very end of law school up until the day he died. He had made a great name for himself in that firm and also with his own criminal law practice and was very excited about finally being out of school and providing for our family.

The events that took place on March 11, 2011—that ended Emmett's life—shattered my family. The night itself was a traumatic event for each of us, and the year and nine months that have followed have brought much heartache and pain.

The decisions made that night that resulted in Emmett being shot in the heart and in the head didn't just end an affair and a life—it ended a family. That gun that was placed in a pocket and driven to Walgreens shot two bullets at a man who was a father. It ended a family.

He was a husband. He was my husband and he was my babies' father. He wasn't always a perfect husband, and sometimes he wasn't a perfect father; but he was ours. He was the man who was greeted every night by ten tiny hands held out waiting for their welcome home hugs. He was the man that sang 'Take me out to the ball game' before bed to his son. He was the leader of our home. He was his little girls' protector and his sons' superhero.

I could spend endless hours typing up painful moments that have shaken the childhood of my five little children. I could type about nights screaming in their beds because they had a dream that a bad guy came into their house and shot them in the head. Nights full of tip toes in my room, followed by tears and questions like, "What if he is still there? What if he is waiting for us and he shoots you too? What if you leave the house and you die … who will love us?" Any time I even stand up to go to another room, five little ones tug on me and break into screams. "Where are you going? Don't leave us. Just sit down."

I could write about Teage's tears shed in a bathroom where a young boy cried while his class performed for their moms and dads celebrating their preschool graduation, sobbing and shaking because he was the only one who didn't have a Dad. He never said one word or sang one note … just sat in a bathroom crying.

I could talk about the thousands and thousands of dollars and time we have spent at therapists and grief counseling groups. I could talk *about Kaleeya and her doggy doggy that Emmett gave her a few weeks before he died. A doggie that now looks like a pile of rags because she won't spend a minute away from him—one of the only lasting memories she has of her father.*

I could type about days where we didn't leave our house because every time we did, fireworks would go off and my kids would almost stop breathing in panic attacks thinking that they heard the gun. Every time an ambulance passes by our house the whole house freezes.

They have endless questions about policemen and why they didn't do their job if they have guns to protect people, "Why didn't they protect my dad?" Twin kindergarteners finally decided to go back to school after their Dad's murder, and I got a call from the school counselor saying my innocent daughters were sitting in her office with broken hearts because some of the boys in their class thought it was cool their Daddy got shot. Weeks later neighbor boys are playing cops and robbers in their front yard and my kids are running inside screaming about a gun that once, as my daughter Bostyn has described many times, "stopped their world".

Nightmares. Endless nightmares. Sometimes even during the day they are afraid to go to sleep that night for fear another nightmare will haunt their dreams. No day has brought my kids back to the normal, carefree childhood days before March 11, 2011.

At least once every day, even still, something reminds one of them of that night. They are reminded that their Dad died lying on the cold concrete of a parking lot. Scared to be alone, but also scared to go to a friend's house or into public. Fear and pain that most kids have never even seen yet on a movie screen. Fear of "the bad guy," fear of reality, anger at a man they never met nor will they ever see.

I teach them forgiveness, hope, and faith in their future, but that doesn't bring back the man who should be sitting by my side and helping his babies through their lives. Years of missed laughs. Millions of missed memories. He didn't see Tytus take his first bite of real food and make that sour face or dance his first dance. He didn't get to see him take his first steps or laugh his first laugh.

Five missed graduations and five missed weddings. He won't be there to walk Kaleeya down the aisle. He will miss the first day of college for Teage. He won't get to sit on the couch with Bostyn and Bailey some day and talk about their first kisses. He will miss it all.

When I pictured the life I always wanted to give my children, I never pictured spending hours every week in a counselor's office listening to them try to put together the pieces that were left of their life. I never pictured sitting them all down and telling them of a decision made by the man that ended the life of their hero.

When I brought these babies into the world, I always pictured that I would be able to protect them and keep them safe at all costs. I always thought that we would live a life of peace and they would never feel the sting that death brings at such a young age in such a horrific way. I certainly never thought I would be teaching my babies what murder is before they knew how to spell it.

The death of Emmett by an angry gunman has taught me that I have no control over the choices others make. It has caused me many days of anxiety and fear. I thought my life in many ways was close to perfect. ... But then it was shattered.

My marriage was ended by a series of bullets as I was sitting at home reading marriage help books and rocking my screaming infant who could feel the same panic I felt that dark night. Little did I know in just a few short hours I wouldn't even have a marriage to help. A marriage that I had worked so hard on and was willing to work on even more was taken from me.

I will never get to sit across a courtroom, as I watched the others involved do, and hear, "I am sorry" and "I still love you!" I will never get to see his face one last time and get answers to the questions that now haunt my dreams. I was robbed of the man whom I had devoted my life to. He was taken from me at the age of thirty. At the age of twenty-eight, I was left a widow with a shattered heart, the reality of the fears I had been seeking answers to, and five babies to raise without their father.

Sitting in that room with the detectives that night, in many ways is a blur. I can remember feeling like I was not able to breathe. I can remember my heart racing and being scared to death to sit my babies down the *next day and tell them what happened.*

A part of me just wanted to pretend he got in a car wreck and turn it into a more simple conversation for my babies, but that was not our reality. Our reality was plain and simple. Our family would never be the same and has never felt the same from that very moment.

Our reality was this: Emmett didn't die because he overcorrected his car or because he forgot to stop at a stop light. Emmett didn't even die because of an affair. Emmett died because of a gun, an angry gunman, and an unforgiving shot to his head and his chest. I wish as the gunman was reminding Emmett of the five kids he had left at home, he himself would have thought about those same five kids as he aimed to pull the trigger.

That decision and that gun have forever changed my children and me. I don't feel like I will ever be whole again. We have picked up the pieces of life and tried to move forward—that is all we had left to do—but there is a void in our lives and in our hearts that will never be replaced. We will try to patch it as the years roll on, but it will never be whole. Like a soldier who loses an eye in combat, we may be able to live and carry on, but it has and will continue to be a hard spot in our lives and in all that we do.

My children lost their childhood, something neither I nor anyone else can ever give them back. They aren't like they used to be, or like other kids are, when it comes to being a carefree kid. They are fearful, they are in pain, and they have been forever hurt.

If only I could have sheltered them and written a different story. But once the past is written, we cannot take it back. They will forever be the sons and daughters of a man who died in a Walgreens parking lot on a cold Friday night in March.

For me, reading those words was so healing. It was a release of so much pain. I got to let those words go that day! It was a moment for which I had been waiting for so long. It was one of the many giant steps that I had to take, another box checked off my list on my road to recovery—on my path to find the purpose of living.

I will never know for sure how those words affected anyone in that room, and frankly, I was finally to a point that it didn't matter. I wasn't reading them in a plea for justice, but in hope that I could find peace as I set them free.

CHAPTER TWELVE

Let It Go

THE TRIAL HAD BEEN OVER for many months. Life was starting to feel normal again in some ways. I was fighting hard every day to see myself. I was overcoming anger and praying for forgiveness. Talk of the past had become less and less; the kids smiled more and more.

It was a normal day: a trip to Costco, cleaning the house, playing with the two little kids while the big ones were at school. Everywhere we were that day Kaleeya kept asking me to play "Let It Go" from *Frozen* on my phone. Though the new song was a usual request around our house, I began to get tired of it on this particular day.

Lunch was over and I carried Tytus upstairs for his nap. As I was leaving his room, I noticed Kaleeya had turned back on her constantly repeated song. I rolled my eyes as I stepped down each stair, thinking, *Isn't there another song we could play?*

As I turned the corner to enter the living room, the music grew louder as it blared from my phone on the floor. I looked over to my little dancer who was standing very still. Tears were falling down her cheeks. She was sobbing.

I fell to my knees in front of her, "Sis, what happened? Are you ok? Are you hurt? What is wrong?"

In the loudest, yet most tender voice I have ever heard, she pleaded for some answers.

She sobbed, "Mommy, I don't understand. Why did he die? Where did he go? I don't know why he died. Why do people *have* to die? It hurts … I just don't get why Daddy Emmett had to die. I don't know where he is or why he isn't here with us anymore. Teage said a bad guy shot him in the night. Is that true? I just don't know why, I don't know … why did he have to die? Why did he have to leave us?"

My heart broke into a million pieces, and for the millionth time I took in a breath as I prayed for answers on what to do. I didn't know what to say. I was stopped, frozen in the moment, trying to comprehend the magnitude of her emotional demands for the truth. The music continued to play, as she stared into my soul for relief from her pain.

For a second I felt trapped—living in a life full of new memories, but being pulled back into the pain—a battle I usually fought alone.

The song still played as her gaze never left mine. Each word entered my ear and pierced another hole in my heart. She had heard the words. The music blaring from the phone took on a whole new meaning as I realized her need for that song was more powerful than the dance. It was way more important than the rhythm or the melody; the words had spoken to her heart.

I scooped up my little girl and rocked her. She put her head on my shoulder, and for the first few seconds, she sobbed like I never knew a little girl could.

Then, without any words to say, I began to sing at the top of my lungs along with the music.

"*Let it gooooooo! Let it gooooooo!*"

Soon Kaleeya's voice joined mine, and we sang those words as if they had been written from our hearts.

A song we had played literally a thousand times that week didn't just make us want to get up and dance or sing along. It had called us to action. And we stood together calling back—pleading for an answer as to how it could be done.

I have had many times when I have cried through a song, but that day I shouted a triumph through my tears, with a little girl who felt broken—a feeling I knew all too well.

The song was on repeat. We spent most of Tytus's naptime singing it over and over, sometimes softly, and sometimes through our tears and shouts of anger, but every time with a plea in our heart that we could learn how to let it go.

I didn't ever again roll my eyes when it started over and voluntarily repeated. I heard the words for the very first time and their truth taught me. Maybe that song was really just about a princess who was learning to let go of her past, but that day it was about a little girl who was learning to stand.

CHAPTER THIRTEEN

The Coat

ONE WINTER DAY DURING THE long months we waited for the looming *Dateline* episode to be filmed, Teage and I were fighting all morning about whether or not he was going to wear his winter coat to school. He said he refused to wear it, and I kept telling him all the reasons why he would. By the time school was about to start and we needed to leave to make it on time, his coat was nowhere to be found.

I was ticked. I just knew he had hidden it from me in order to get his way and not have to wear it to school. I let him have it and told him how embarrassing it was to send him to school without a coat, how every other mom would be judging my parenting, and all the teachers were going to talk about how bad of a mother I was.

By the time we got to school he didn't even say goodbye—just slammed his door and ran out onto the playground. I was frustrated. Not so much because he slammed the door, or he was going to be cold, but because he won. He didn't have to wear his coat because it was nowhere to be found. I had to give in because he had tricked me into losing. I was the victim.

I drove home pissed off. I got Kaleeya and Tytus out of the car and went into the house. Soon my phone was ringing.

It was Shawn and he was a bit hysterical. He said, "Ash, a bus got in a crash not far from my work and a little boy was killed. He was good friends with one of my employee's sons. It breaks my heart."

As he was explaining the events that had taken place, I had sat down on the couch. In the middle of our conversation, I glanced over to the kitchen table and right under the chair Teage had been sitting in for breakfast was his lost coat.

I hung up the phone and burst into tears. A little boy had died in our town. *What if that would have been one of ours? What if that would have been Teage? What if the last conversation I had with my son that morning was a fight about a winter coat and me blaming him for lying to me? What if Teage had slammed his door and not kissed me and then he died?*

I put the little ones back in the car and drove straight to the school. With his coat in my hand, I asked the office to call Teage up to meet me. As he rounded the corner tears fell from my eyes again.

I held out his coat and said, "Son, I am so sorry. This morning I blamed you for lying to me and you didn't. I fought with you about wearing your winter coat so I could look like a good mom. I acted like an idiot, and I let you leave without kissing me goodbye. I am so sorry. I don't care if you wear this coat. I don't expect you to always follow my counsel. I just want you to know I love you and that no matter what happens today, you know that the most important thing is you."

He threw his arms around me and for a minute didn't let go. It wasn't about the coat or who was right—all that mattered to me that day was that my son knew he was loved in case I never got to tell him again.

We aren't always going to be reminded that there will come a final morning with our loved ones. It is moments like these that make us want to slow down just a little bit and see all the blessings in our lives.

Those last words and final goodbyes aren't always on the forefront of our minds, but maybe if they were, we would make them count a little bit more.

It isn't the coats our children wear that determine if we are good parents, but the love we give when we remember it is *them* that make us great.

Not all goodbyes will be our last, but I am not sure I want to take a chance not saying the most important things. So the next time a moment of frustration leaves me feeling like I have lost a fight, I hope to remember there is more to lose than an insignificant battle.

Lose a few battles if it means gaining a little bit of love. Someday when that love is gone, you may wish you had let it win.

It isn't always about winning the battle, but remembering what we are fighting for. Let us always remember: the best gifts are found in our hearts.

CHAPTER FOURTEEN

Dateline

AFTER MONTHS OF WAITING, THE day came: my interview with *Dateline*.

I walked into that room with my head held high. Keith Morrison and I talked for three hours. It was just like the victim impact statement, only with no limitations on what I could or could not say—just me, telling our story.

We cried together. We laughed. And for the first time, I told it all. I talked about the details of the darkest day of my life. And as I walked away, it almost felt like it hurt a little less.

Then we waited again. This time wondering every day how our story was going to be portrayed by *Dateline NBC*.

It is a weird feeling watching yourself on TV, let alone watching yourself cry your face off in every scene while telling a story you never thought you would share. But I did. And once the TV was turned off, I thought it was over! The story. The pain. The memories. I was ready to close a chapter of the darkest years of my existence.

I felt free. I wasn't sure how I felt about some of the facts shared on the show. I had no idea of the hundreds of people I would meet every time I left my house, feeling like they knew me from somewhere. For me it was finally "over." So that day, I celebrated freedom.

That night I went to bed feeling like I could breathe for the first time in years.

I had an intriguing dream. I was walking along the edge of a cliff. There was water raging far beneath my feet. I could hear the ocean hitting against the wall. I could almost smell the scent of the salty water. Soon I looked down and in my hand, I found a book. It was my story—all the parts that *Dateline* had not shown.

I knew the minute I saw the cover the truths that it held inside. All my secret pain. All the days I spent staring out the window into the darkness, honestly believing that was the only answer to protecting what I had left of my family. All the darkest parts of my pain—the ones nobody would ever hear. The worthless girl who had never come out of hiding.

Soon the ocean beckoned, and I took my arm and wound it up behind me. I threw that book as far as I could towards the water. I watched it as it sailed through the sky, its pages flowing in the wind. And then the coolest thing happened: It hit the water and sank.

I woke up sure that dream was a symbolism of the closing of a chapter—the ending of our story. Little did I know on that morning as I celebrated the silence I thought I was being blessed to finally find, God had a different plan.

CHAPTER FIFTEEN

Proceed to the Route

ONE SUMMER WHILE DRIVING THROUGH Utah, we ran into some road construction. The detour caused us to have to ride on the other side of a widely divided highway. My phone began to panic. Siri kept yelling, "Proceed to the route! Proceed to the route!!!" as loud as I have ever heard her speak. She knew something was wrong. The route I had asked her to guide me to was not the one I seemed to be following. To my phone, I was traveling on the wrong side of a one-way highway.

It almost scared me how persistent my GPS was that I was headed down the wrong course. It caused me to reflect upon my actions and ponder all the turns I had taken. At one point I even stopped and asked a stranger outside of a gas station if I was on the right course. It turned out I was still very far away from my destination, but had been on the right path to get there.

I don't know how many times in my life I have felt like I have taken a wrong turn. There have been many occasions when I have had to slow down and reflect upon the course I have taken to lead me to where I was. I have questioned some of my turns, as they have brought me to some pretty rocky roads.

But other times, no matter who has told me, I was on the wrong path, I knew I was right where I was supposed to be. Life is strange—each one is so very unique.

Each year, as one year turns into the next, I have paused to reflect on where I have been, but even more on where I am headed and where I want to end up.

In January 2014, I was having one of the biggest internal battles of my life. I had spent Friday night in the temple and had received the strongest prompting to start blogging about my journey. I wrestled with that feeling all weekend long. I didn't say a word to anyone about it. I was cross and snappy. I was scared and felt so alone.

I was in a depression just thinking about opening up and sharing the deepest pains of my heart, and I could not talk the rational side of my brain into believing this would be a good path for me.

By Monday night it was so bad I got a priesthood blessing. In the blessing I heard the same words I had in the temple: "I need you to be a voice to others of my children who aren't listening. They are hurting too."

The next day a blog was born.

At first I thought I was being given an opportunity to lash out in hate—to tell anyone who ever stumbled across my story how much it hurt. I thought God was giving permission to write about a victim of a crime. I typed like my life depended on it. I sat there for hours, writing the story of three people who had ruined my life. Soon my computer shut down. I frantically turned it back on and scrambled to the blog. Not a word was saved. The post was blank, nothing had auto saved. I could almost hear God gently guide me forward urging me to start over with a different view.

So I began again. This time with a prayer that I could see what I was missing.

As the words filled the page and the tears fell like rain, I was blessed with a different view. This wasn't going to be the tale of a victim; it was going to be the stories of how we survived. The moments of grace. The moments we were able to stand.

There it was, my name. These words came out on the screen as I typed—*"The Moments We Stand."*

When I went to push publish on the first post, I paused for a few minutes. I remember praying so hard with bullheaded tears falling down my cheeks, "Heavenly Father, I don't know why I am supposed to do this. I don't understand how this is going to help me and the kids. But I have faith that the one person who needs this will find it. I pray that it can make a difference for them.

"I don't really want to do this. I am scared to share so much humiliation and heartache, but I do this for *You*. I dedicate this blog to my children who will one day need to hear the stories it will hold, but only because You have asked me to.

"I have been carried by angels. I have seen Your hand in my life every single day. I have faith that You are putting me on the right course. Please let anyone in pain who reads these stories find hope in Christ."

Chills covered my body. I felt so much love surrounding me. I knew what I had to do. I clicked publish.

~ ~ ~

If you would have told me, even weeks before that very minute, that this journey would have been mine, I would have shrugged my shoulders and laughed. There has been little about this journaling mission that has been fun for me, but it has brought me so much joy. I have so powerfully felt, for the first time since Emmett died, that I am on the right course.

Yes, there have been others who have tried to tell me I am doing this for a purpose different than I am. There have been many with cruel opinions about who they think I am, and that is OK.

If there is one thing I have learned, it is this: when God believes in you—or asks you to be more than you are on your own—you grab His hand and follow. You don't wait around to see who thinks it is a good idea or ask for the support of anyone but Him. You merely have faith that the right GPS is the one telling you to get back on the right path.

Sometimes God is whispering, "Proceed to the route." (Sometimes He has to shout it quite loud—especially for me!) And sometimes He is merely sticking you on a trail He needs you to be on.

Faith, as scary as it is, is what brings us to find our missions.

My blog has not just been an amazing outlet of the pain and anger from my heart, as I thought it would be when I started that January. It has saved me from myself. It has helped me remember all the truths I have known all along.

It has given me an opportunity to remember the good times I had before the murder, and to look forward to the ones that lay ahead. It has been an opportunity for me to reflect upon my relationship with God and the foundation He has been in every single day of my life.

It is strange to look back on certain days that I once felt were as black as night and remember all the tender mercies that have been a light to help me find my way through them. Sometimes in the moment, tender mercies seem to be mere coincidences. Sometimes for me, it isn't until I look back upon them that I truly see Heavenly Father's hand.

I am grateful for everyone who has cheered me along (though the first time I got a comment from a stranger I almost shut the whole thing down). The kind words and tender stories have been a huge support to help me remember why this was the path I was supposed to take.

For all those years I felt so alone—I cannot feel so now. There is a whole world of quiet pain, each one unique. Maybe your answer will not be to share publicly how it has felt for you, but please know you are not alone. Heavenly Father is always on your side. Our older brother Jesus Christ has shared with Him every pain you feel and every fight you have battled.

So as you reflect upon your story of the years gone by—look for the times when He was there for *you*. As you look to the future, pray that the course you are walking is for Him. Maybe others will tell you to "proceed to the route," but the only trail worth traveling is the one being paved by God.

I hope this year will be the best this world has seen. I pray there will be more love and we will be able to better serve one another. I hope we will think a little more before we speak, and we may love before we hate. I wish for peace, healing, and hope for all.

But even more than all of this, I pray for each of us to feel God's love. When things are going your way, and even when you are flat on your face, pray to be able to see yourself how He sees you and you will feel joy.

If you have lost your way, now is your time to "proceed to the route." This life isn't over until it is over. If you are standing at a crossroads and have forgotten what trail you were trying to follow, seek the right guidance to help you proceed back to the route where you will be able to protect and be protected.

Not all crossroads are a battle of right and wrong, but each path we follow will lead us to the next. Protect the dreams you are already living, but don't doubt yourself when you are asked to proceed to the next trail. Each of us will have a unique route to conquer, but only you can know which trails were meant to be followed.

Sometimes I feel as insignificant as I did the day I started this healing journey as I pour my heart out with memories of the past, but many things have changed: I am remembering who I always have been, I am embracing my story, I am seeking truth, and I am finding hope every day.

I still occasionally battle the temptation to doubt that I am enough. Sometimes I still fight the dark fears that try to creep in and destroy everything I know to be true. But one thing is for sure: for every time I fall, I am still finding reasons to stand. And I know you can too.

CHAPTER SIXTEEN

Stranger

AFTER POSTING FOR THE FIRST time on the blog, I decided I would go on Facebook and Instagram and let my friends and family know of my new adventure. I said something along the lines of, "I am going to start to journal our healing journey on a blog if anyone wants to follow along."

I had every intention of doing a few posts that my mom and sister would read and then calling it a day. Within a week, one million people had visited my blog. The first comment I received from a stranger almost caused me to shut the whole thing down.

Each night as I would work on the next post, I would pour my heart out through my tears. Partly because of the hard story I was journaling about, but mainly for the hard thing I felt God was asking me to do.

I begged in my prayers almost every night for the first six months for it to all be over. I started receiving emails daily from strangers telling me how much my vulnerability was helping them heal in their own journey. I pleaded every night that God would find someone more worthy of "helping others" as the emails had said.

Each day I wrote a little bit more. And each post I started to remember truths about myself that had been lost along the way. Soon, emails began to remind me that my words were giving people light. I knew the truth: they had come from God to me as a gift to help me heal. It had nothing to do with me, and everything to do with Him.

Then one day someone asked me to step even more outside my comfort zone and speak at a single's conference. I agreed.

For weeks leading up to the event, my fears surrounded me. My cousin Tiffanie even joked, "Ash, are they sure they want *you* to speak for this conference. Won't your story scare these poor singles out of wanting to ever get married?!"

We had a good laugh, but she was right. What did I have to offer anyone? I felt like a fraud.

That day, as I was in the middle of a breakdown, feeling overwhelmed and under qualified and as I was looking through my nightstand for another resource to use in my talk, I came across something I hadn't seen for a while: Emmett's patriarchal blessing (a blessing each individual can get in my church that offers us guidance in our own personal lives).

I read each word on the paper as tears fell down my face. A few words in particular stuck out to me: *Emmett, you must leave a great legacy for your posterity.*

A bitterness filled my heart, and for a split second I felt sorry for the man who was given this blessing. He didn't get that chance. How was part of his mission on this earth to leave a great legacy for his family if he died during his lowest days? For the thousandth time, in my mind, I screamed at a man and a gun.

You took this from him! On his worst day, you robbed him of his chance to leave the legacy he was promised to leave. He won't get to make a difference in anyone's life. He is gone. And he will never fulfill this promise. His legacy is worth nothing. Rob, you and that gun made it so he doesn't even get the chance to leave the legacy he was supposed to leave for our children.

I read the line over and over again and the tears continued to fall. Then all of the sudden, I felt a calm surrounding me, and I heard as plain as day, "Every time you tell my story, *you* will leave the legacy for our posterity. Tell them everything, even if it only saves just one. As they heal, so will you … and so will I."

I was on a mission—not just for myself, but for a man who had some unfinished business. A man who needed just as much healing as I did, but had been taken before he could find it for himself. A man who needed to leave a legacy that would change the world, even for just one person.

I never once doubted again the purpose of my vulnerability. I was still scared, and felt very alone, but I knew that it was all part of a greater plan.

I promised Emmett a long time ago that I would walk by him through thick and thin. He hasn't always made that very easy, but I know without a doubt he is trying to make it right.

And that is what forgiveness is to me every single day. Taking the pain and the journey and the fear and letting it all go. Not because it all the sudden feels better, but because I am not really living with it all stuck inside me.

I am a victim of three people's horrible choices. But when I choose another way—the survivor—I get to be me again. Not the same girl from before the gun fire—one who is way stronger. One who has to fight every day to love. One who has to choose to stand over and over again.

Since the day I published my first post on my blog, it has had over 11 million readers. I have had hundreds of interviews with media and TV stations. Our story has been on *Fox News*, *Deseret News*, *KTVB 7's Hero*, UK magazines, *True Crime Daily*, *Sex and Murder*, *American Monster*, podcasts, and many more. I even went on *Dr. Phil*.

A few years ago, I was asked in an interview on a podcast a question that really made me think. The question was this: "What would you say your greatest accomplishment has been? *Dateline*, the blog, *Dr. Phil*, your books, your healing trauma conferences—out of all the things you have done over the last few years, what would you say has been your greatest accomplishment?"

I thought for a minute over all that I had "accomplished" by telling our story. And then it hit me, "I would have to say my greatest accomplishment is finding my worth. It was the hardest thing I have done after living through all that I have, but it is the one thing I will never stop fighting for. Knowing I have value and am enough, no matter what my story is."

So that has become my focus. I used to think I stood on stages to save just one from using a gun when words would do the job, from having an affair, from walking out on his or her family. But now I tell a story about a horrific, humiliating journey, because it was through it and the battles that followed that I found out who I was all along: a woman full of strength, gifts, talents, and truth.

As I have cleared away the darkness that once settled in my soul, I have found the truths that were hidden way down deep. I am enough. I have worth and value and a mission I was sent to earth to fulfill. I am not the victim in chains as I once thought I would always be. I am free. Free to choose happiness. Free to choose life. And free to choose who I will become.

This story did not break me, and yours doesn't have to break you either. We were born for greatness. We were born to find our truths, and we each have a unique journey that leads us to the low points that help us remember how to fight to find our way out of them again.

What is your story? Who are you forgetting? Are you going to be that girl (or boy) surrounded by the chains of victimhood or are you going to be the one on the other side of the coin who knows the truth? One is a lie, and one is your freedom. So who is it going to be?

I choose me. I choose to live, not in the chains of victimhood, but in the freedom of grace. He never once left me, and for the first time in my story I truly know that He never will. A victim is acted upon. A survivor who is connected to the Savior acts for Him.

Our stories are enough for His grace. You are enough for His love.

CHAPTER SEVENTEEN

Dr. Phil

THERE IS MUCH I COULD share about going on *Dr. Phil*. Here is the simple version: go watch the dramatized watered-down version of what it became online.

Dr. Phil's people had been contacting me for months. I told them "NO!" a few times, but on the fourth time, I told them I would think about it. As I thought and prayed about what to do, I felt impressed to go on the show and share my heart.

My idea and God's version of what became of that show were definitely not the same. You see, I pictured it like this: Ashlee on the stage with Dr. Phil sharing light. Talking about the lessons I learned through the pain of my story. Sharing details about my book and why I didn't write the details of the murder, but the emotions I felt each and every day.

I pictured us talking about my *A Reason to Stand* conferences. The nonprofit. I pictured it ending with a nice, not too long hug from Dr. Phil, a pat on the back, and a small "atta boy" as they clapped me off stage.

Do you know why I pictured it this way? That's right, because that is the picture that was painted in every email and phone call. A stepping stool for me to spread my light, a moment of triumph to celebrate how much I had overcome and how I had turned it into something to help others.

Here is the difference between what happened on that show and what I thought it was going to be. I was again surrounded by darkness. A place I thought was going to be safe became another traumatic moment in my journey. A "doctor" that promised to help me heal caused me more pain.

I left that show in a state of shock that began the minute I was backstage before the filming and they showed a clip of "my story." It started out something like this, "*Two women ...*" And it didn't end much differently.

I didn't know Kandi was going to be on that stage with me. I was not prepared to have her attack me from multiple angles and on every topic. I didn't even want to be on that stage when Maury—I mean Dr. Phil—turned the tables and began attacking her. None of it was healing for me.

So as the limo drove me back to the hotel where my family was playing in the pool waiting for me, I couldn't even cry. I was so blown away with the chaos that had just blown up in my face. I felt trapped—tricked—not just by Dr. Phil and the producers, but by God. How could He do this to me? I prayed so hard about the decision. So why was I played the fool?

The PTSD that once seemed to be on the mend returned that day on a whole new level. I began not sleeping again. I stared out the window at night into the darkness at nothing. I was afraid of everything. I didn't want to leave my house.

And do you know what caused the most pain? I still needed her. At least I believed I did. I needed her to be sorry so I could feel better about myself. They did try to make it look like she said sorry, by cutting different scenes of us on the stage, but in the uncut version, she was just cruel. Everything was made to look how they wanted it to look, and everything I actually said that could have been healing was deleted.

So for about a month I couldn't snap out of it. Then one day I decided to ask God why. I had written a whole book about faith, then all the sudden I was doubting mine. So I went where I do—into my closet—and fell to my knees.

I cried out, "Why did you do that to me? Why would you let her hurt me again? Can't you see how bad that hur? Why would you want me to go back to this?"

And then I waited in silence for what seemed like a lifetime. And then in my heart I felt this truth, "Ashlee, you don't need her to heal. I needed you to know that without a doubt. I need you to know that you are *strong*."

Strong? You think I am strong? How? What on earth have I done that proves to anyone I have strength? Show me how I have been strong.

All at once I could see that day, sitting on the stage across from what some might call my greatest enemy. Face to face. I always dreamed of a moment like that. I always thought my healing would come from an opportunity to lash out. Kandi would be so humbled that she'd say how sorry she was and how she just wishes she could take it back. She'd acknowledge everything we had been through because of her and her husband and Emmett.

I thought my healing would come as I yelled and screamed and got it all out—and there that moment was, like it had come straight from the gods. Dr. Phil had created the perfect moment for me to use my ability to throw up unfiltered hatred to a person who was so deserving of it in my eyes. I had waited for a moment like this since the moment that gun had sounded.

But God showed me a different kind of strength that day. The strength He gave me was way greater than the bullheaded kind I had used so much in the past. As I knelt in my closet, He showed me all the reasons why I went on that show. And since that moment on my knees, I have truly seen what forgiveness looks like. It had nothing to do with her, and everything to do with Him.

So though I can't say that Dr. Phil and I have become great friends, I am so thankful for everything he didn't know he was doing for me that day. He gave me the opportunity the world had told me I needed so I could have the moment that Heavenly Father knew would change me.

Sometimes healing comes in the most unique ways. Our strength is shown to us by showing up in a way we never imagined it would. When the world tells us to puff up, sometimes God shows us how to keep it classy.

I love this quote by Patrick Weaver:

> Your calling is going to crush you. If you're called to mend the brokenhearted, you're going to wrestle with brokenheartedness. If you're called to prophesy, you're going to struggle to control your mouth. If you're called to lay hands, you will battle spiritual viruses. If you are called to preach and to teach the gospel, you will be sifted for the wisdom that anoints your message. If you are called to empower, your self-esteem will be attacked, your successes will be hard-fought. Your calling will come with cups, thorns, and sifting that are necessary for your mantle to be authentic, humble and powerful. Your crushing won't be easy because your assignment is not easy. Your oil is not cheap.

We have all been called to this earth for a reason. We will all come to crossroads and carry burdens that we do not understand. We will all face times when we will wonder if God doesn't see us or if he sees us as stronger than we believe we are.

So when life gets strange and you doubt if He sees you at all or wonder if He sees more than you feel worthy of, just don't forget that He might be calling you to do something greater. He might see a strength you didn't know possible. He might be asking you to get stronger for the next rocky road your strength will have to carry you through.

You are capable. You are enough. Don't hold it back, unless that is the skill He is asking you to work on. Then hold it back in the new kind of strength He is sending. Sometimes not saying the words you could adequately fire is a curse, and sometimes it is the greatest gift you never knew you would need.

To Dr. Phil and all of his friends at that network, thank you for trying to set me up to explode so I could learn how to stay composed. I didn't need her, but I sure did need me. You helped me find me again.

You might have made a lot of money off my pain that day. Good for you. I know what I walked away with was worth way more.

Some of the greatest gifts we are given are in the moments we think we are weak. Finding our strength always takes having it challenged. Becoming our best selves is a goal we will start to find as we walk through the dark and fight for the light.

CHAPTER EIGHTEEN

Too Close to the Fence

I HAVE ANOTHER STORY I want to share before we get into the work part of this book.

It all started November 1, 2017. Our four girls were off at activities and the boys and their friends were jumping on the trampoline and playing in the grass with our dog Sadie. My friend and I were talking as we watched the kids run around in the backyard.

Sadie, as she usually does, began running along the fence line playing with the neighbor's two German shepherds. It was an activity I had always encouraged in hopes of getting her at least five minutes of exercise each day. She always got a rush of energy when they were running the fence with her. I had always just assumed they were her only friends, and I think she did too.

For the millionth time, on her own side of the fence, Sadie got a jolt of energy and booked it down the fence line, playing their usual game. Prepared to run a race she would never win, be defeated, go back inside, and fall asleep on the couch. It was the same every time … until that day.

Sadie was only half-way down the fence line when all of the sudden she appeared to be stuck on something. At first I didn't comprehend what was happening, but as I ran towards the commotion of Teage's panicked cry and dogs making noises, I could see that the two German shepherds had both stuck their noses between the slats in the fence and were clamped down with their jaws tight on our dog, their bodies still in their own yard. They began to try to pull her in opposite directions through the slits between the wrought iron posts.

I knew at that moment she was gone. She wasn't making a noise as one of the dogs was pretty much clamping down on her airway and her eyes were rolled back in her head. But I also knew I wasn't going to let them destroy her body any more than it already was in front of my babies. So I did what any mama bear would do. I decided to fight.

In complete shock, Teage and I began punching, kicking, yelling, and crying … begging these animals to set her free. To no avail Sadie was still being pulled through two separate openings she would never fit through by two different mouths.

I began to scream at the top of my lungs, hoping for anyone around to come and help me set her free so we could give her a proper burial. Soon, a few neighbors came running to the rescue. It took 3 adults and one ten-year-old punching and kicking for a few minutes to get the other dogs to let her go, and once they did, she took a breath.

She was still alive! Mangled, bleeding, and full of holes and shaking with fear, but alive.

The whole left side of her body was covered in blood and teeth marks—some so deep you could see her insides. Sadie got a lot of stitches that night. The doctor in the ER vet clinic said her extra fat saved her life (A lesson we might want to consider. "I am eating for my safety!"). Then, with the help of some miracle worker doctors, she was sent home to recover the very next morning.

For someone who has suffered with PTSD for all those years, I can't say I didn't fall into a state of intense fear most of that night. The "Why us? Why my son who already struggles with fear of the unknown?" ate at me for the hours I sat waiting.

I ran the gamut on victim pity parties in my mind. I quickly went through the grief cycle as I waited in a room for hours to see if the dog I bought for my kids as a therapy healing animal was going to make it. And I sobbed even harder the next morning when she came home with a heartbeat, but looked like she wished she was dead.

I cried for her pain and for the struggle I feared this moment of trauma was going to cause in the lives of my already hurting children. I struggled with a belief racked in fear that has tried to haunt me many times before. *I do not have the ability to protect them.* The evidence had never felt so strong as this scene had played out in the safety of our own property while I stood by.

I know now that those fears that came into my mind as I thought I was failing yet again aren't true. So I want to share a few things I have learned from this moment of fear.

#1. We are not promised tomorrow. Literally the day before, I said out loud and on Instagram how grateful I am for such a perfect dog. I thought at that moment those words left my lips that maybe she was God's way of blessing us for all the hell we have been through.

Then, not even twenty-four hours later, I thought we had lost her forever. Not because of anything we did or did not do, but because life is full of bumps in the road and fences we must not walk too close to.

#2. There are going to be "German shepherds" in our lives. Obviously I am not talking about the breed. There are many of these dogs that have saved lives and been lifelong companions for people.

I am talking about traumatic moments—someone or something coming out of nowhere and tearing you down. Some we might not ever see coming. Some are merely the voices we hear in our minds threatening us to just give up. Some are going to be real life bad guys with guns. Others might be threats to our marriages, or bullies at school.

Whatever our "German shepherds" have been or will be, they are unique to each of us individually. They can either cause us to give up or they can give us a reason to fight—a reason to stand a little taller.

#3. Sometimes we might not see the wolves in sheep's clothing, and we learn through a lot of pain that some don't want to be the friend we hoped they were. Other times we might gain a friend in someone we thought was out to get us.

#4. Sometimes—just like Daniel in the Bible—we will be thrown into a lion's den. Sometimes God will calm the lions, and other times He will send a miracle in a different way. On this day in my backyard, I saw hundreds of miracles.

#5. We cannot walk too close to the fence. There are some things in this world that just make sense. We can clearly see the consequences of walking along the edge of a cliff because we can easily see what can go wrong. But how many situations do we encounter each day where the outcomes are not as clear?

If there is something in your life that you keep taking a risk for that maybe isn't really going to be worth it in the end, take a few steps back. It just might save your life.

#6. No matter how hard we work, or how much money we spend to help someone heal, we don't get to decide how they will receive it. We cannot force them to accept our "love" and our "knowledge" of what is best for them.

Sadie was stitched up from head to toe. She didn't eat much for days. She hardly moved at all. But once she started healing and those stitches started itching, she decided, one day, to use her back leg to not only dig out her stitches but to reopen the biggest wound she had received from her attack. Blood everywhere again. More pain.

#7. If we want to heal, we can't keep reopening our wounds. We have to let others do their jobs to help us. We have to let stitches heal before we try to take them out ourselves. Some things take time. And though at the moment, it may seem to feel good to make some hurt again, they aren't worth digging back up.

#8. Some fences are not built well enough to keep the darkness out. But some of the fences and walls we create for ourselves are the very things that are not letting the light in.

There have been other "German shepherds" and fences that should have been avoided. What you don't know is that a few months after poor Sadie was attacked at the fence, I again stood at a crossroad where I had to choose.

Shawn became the do-over I had prayed so hard for in my closet on the night of Emmett's death. I found myself pleading for my worth and fighting to know what to do. This time God gave me the chance to choose the ending. Sitting at the temple for weeks the answer was the same, "It is time for you to go. You are worth more than both of these men could see."

Divorce? It didn't seem real. How could His answer to a husband being unfaithful be to give up? My fears kicked in and I struggled for weeks to listen.

I always said if I had the chance I would have stood by Emmett's side and we would have walked hand in hand to our future together. He would have picked me, and I him. We would have worked through his infidelity and walked away stronger. My do-over came, not with Emmett, but in an almost identical story, and God told me to go.

In the back of my mind all along I had pictured Emmett losing his chance to pick me by his murder, but the truth is Emmett did have a choice long before he died. For seven years he could—and should—have placed me at the highest point and pedestal of his life, but he didn't. He chose and died fighting for her.

So today I plead with you—those who have the ability to take a step back. Run. Find fences and company that are worth living for and are not posing as a friend in a safe backyard. Put your family first always.

Our relationships, our decisions, our integrity—they matter. Don't walk too close to the fence. Decide now what side you want to be on, and don't let anyone try to pull you through to the other side. First of all, you don't fit. Second of all, the grass isn't always greener over there, and the aftermath of your choices is not something you get to choose.

And when those "German shepherds" come—and they will come—just don't forget who you are. It isn't what we go through, but what we become after the pain that makes all the difference. Yes, we may carry scars and have wounds we are tempted to open up again and again, but we can heal.

If you feel like you have been attacked, belittled, humiliated, and the "German shepherds" around you seem to have forgotten your worth, don't you dare give up. You aren't broken. You have so much yet to live for. The world still needs you. And as you heal those fears of all the moments you were not shown the love you deserve, just remember: you are still enough—broken and all.

Sometimes we trust and get hurt anyway. It doesn't mean we didn't do our best. Having faith in a plan, and having that plan fail us does not have to be evidence of our worthlessness, or a reason for us to lose faith in others. For every "dog" that has attacked, there is another that has brought love and companionship. For every plan that has changed and failed, there is a plan that has changed and brought so much success and even joy.

We have to be there for each other. God doesn't send us one another by accident. An animal that was brought to our family to be a therapy dog was now taking her turn teaching us how to be her "therapy people." The circle of life doesn't always have to bring death.

Healing isn't easy, but it is possible. So, Sadie, thanks for being strong—for fighting for another day. For reminding me *again* how I need to make the most of every moment and never take advantage of all I have been given. Also, thanks for showing these kids how to fight and giving them a new hope that not every attack ends in death.

Today as you assess the fences you walk, just remember that as wounds heal, the pain does too. If you are holding on to the pain of a wound that has long since healed physically, maybe today it is time to stop digging in and letting it hurt you emotionally or mentally. Ask for the help you need. There are people who can help you stitch it up once and for all. You will see miracles as you pray for grace.

Life is too hard to do it alone. We need each other. And we don't just need each other's presence—we need each other's love. Perfectly imperfect love.

Don't walk too close to the fence, but don't be afraid to make room on your side for the people who need you the most.

He never said it would be easy … just worth it.

CHAPTER NINETEEN

A Few Hard Days Then Faith in the Plan

THERE WAS A TIME WHEN I thought I had this life thing all figured out. I followed the list—the one I thought I had to obey in order to receive everything I wanted in the order and way I wanted it.

And life kind of played out according to that plan … until it didn't. I thought I had seen it all living through betrayal trauma and a murder on the same day. I thought I had been through all my hard battles. I thought life was going to go smoothly from there on out until it didn't.

I did everything in my power to keep me from "losing" again. And then one day Heavenly Father told me I needed to be done fighting. How? After seven years of promising I would have stood by Emmett's side and fought for our marriage through anything, I was standing in a similar place and getting a different answer. It was like Heavenly Father was saying, "I know you always said you would have stayed, but now I need you to have faith and show me that you trust me. I need you to leave."

For seven years I had judged those who still had a husband living and walked away. To be honest, parts of me had come to believe that divorce was the coward's way out. I truly thought in the back of my mind that they were just giving up. I prayed many times for answers to why these women had a chance to make things right with their husbands and mine was taken away. Why would they just leave?

I am humbled to say that I was wrong. For months I fought it, afraid to fail. And then one day proved it was time to go. As I have heard many women describe, and as I now know for myself, divorce is sometimes God's answer to our prayers. It is just as brave as staying, just a different kind.

With the same leap of faith required of us to love, sometimes God asks us to move forward in ways we never thought possible or right. He asks us to bravely walk away from something He once gave us strength to fight for. Sometimes the things that feel like a curse are really a blessing.

Blessed? Yes. Answers from our Heavenly Father, though they don't always make sense at the moment, are always right.

I know some of you are thinking, "Yeah sure God told you to get divorced. I am sure He wants to break up families." And that's OK. I have thought that many times too in the past. And hopefully one day you won't have to go through such a humbling lesson as I have. But what I want you to know is that God has a plan for each of us, and they all look different. And that is beautiful.

Today I want to tell you some of the stories of the blessings that have followed my leap of faith to move forward—again—down a different path than I had planned.

It started the night I knew I had to get divorced. I left Teage's basketball game with a car full of five kids, not sure where we were going to sleep that night. My heart hurt, but I was full of peace. I texted my sisters and asked them to meet at Ali's house. My brother-in-law Will gave me a blessing. In more than one way the blessing told me that I was going to have a few really hard days, and then I needed to have faith in the plan. That was one thing I knew I could do.

The next month was full of some really hard days—some a little scary. Finally, the divorce was final and the kids and I got to move back into the house. The next weekend, my friend Alesha Penland came to visit with her cute daughter.

If her name sounds familiar to you, it may be because she has told her story a few times at *A Reason to Stand*, and on my Facebook account. She lives in Utah and her infant son Lincoln was killed four years ago at a daycare center. She and I actually became friends through email after Lincoln's murder and met for the first time at the Ogden *A Reason to Stand* conference a few months later.

On her way up, Alesha called and said, "OK, I have been thinking all day, and when I was in the temple this morning, I kept thinking of you and this nice guy who lives across the street from me. You have nothing keeping you in Idaho and lots of reasons why you should move to Utah. What if you could meet a good guy here? Just going to throw that out there. I think you should move to Utah."

I replied, totally joking, "Haha, yeah. Maybe someday. You know what? Yeah, OK. You tell that guy about me. I am sure he is one who would want a divorced widow with five kids."

Then she practically jumped through the phone and giddily said, "You know what? Oh my gosh, that's what I am supposed to do. This guy who lives by me and goes to my church, yeah, I am supposed to set you up with him."

I started laughing, "Guy. Haha, *no*. I was just kidding. I am not doing that whole dating thing for a *long* time. I was totally joking, and super not interested in dating anyone, like ever."

She didn't let it go. The whole weekend she talked about this friend of her husband's named Scott who lived in her neighborhood. "He is thirty-nine, has never been married. He is the Elders Quorum president in our ward; he is like the nicest guy I know. I know he has dated like a lot, but has saved himself for the right one. Seriously, you have to come visit me and meet him."

Finally I said, "Honestly, he sounds hideous, but maybe when I am ready I will humor you and come and meet him someday."

Sunday morning she left my house and by Monday night I got a text from her neighbor Scott. A few days later we talked on the phone. Every night that week we stayed up late talking and laughing, and by the weekend he was driving to Idaho to take me on a real date.

You bet I was nervous. That day I checked in with my widow group and told them I had a date. They reminded me that I had made a vow to them that I would kiss at least ten guys before I could officially start dating anyone. I laughed at the thought. I didn't plan on dating anyone seriously for at least a year or two.

And then there was a knock at my door. My date, who had traveled four hours, was here. He was adorable—way cuter than any of the pictures Alesha had shown me the weekend before. And he smelled amazing.

We didn't have a quiet moment the whole night. We laughed and talked until midnight like we had known each other for years. He told me the stories of dating for twenty years, and I told him my story of being a divorced widow with five kids—which ironically he had seen on TV a few times. Our paths were so very different, but we had so much in common. We had so much fun together.

And the next day was the same. And so was the next day after that.

So every weekend he made the trek to take me out. Everything was so natural, and the minute he met the kids, they took him right in. He felt like a missing piece to a puzzle we had given up hope of completing.

At the end of February, the kids and I decided to drive his way. We went to a Jazz game and took a train down to temple square. We got to meet a few of his siblings and his parents. They were all so loving and made us feel right at home.

One night his brother-in-law Chris pulled me aside while we were all cleaning up dinner and said, "OK, you want to know the truth about Scott?" I was thinking, *Oh finally someone is going to tell me why this amazing guy is still single.*

He continued, "I have been in this family for thirteen years, and every time I hang out with Scott I think, 'How the hell is this guy not married?' He is the coolest guy I know, and we kind of always just figured God was saving him for someone great and we all hope that it is you."

Every week I fell a little more in love with him. Every night we talked on the phone until the early hours of the morning, and every weekend we got to see each other. He would come down and stay at my neighbor's or we would go to see him.

We met up in Bear Lake for Emmett's grandma's 90th birthday and he met all of Emmett's family. I think the moment I fell the most in love with him was watching him stand by Emmett's graveside with us while he asked Emmett's mom about everything on the grave and all the nicknames she had for him and her favorite memories of when Emmett was a kid.

You never think when you are a kid you will ever have to stand at the grave of the man you created five kids with and hope that another man will be able to be confident enough to know you have a whole part of your life he wasn't a part of, but he can still love you.

That weekend Scott showed me what that looked like. And I can say, it takes a real man to do this job. Those of you stepping in after death or divorce and loving, you are a brave and noble group of individuals. I can't say I could do it so empathetically and with so much honor. But you do. Thank you.

Another weekend we met in Las Vegas for the twins' birthday and an *A Reason to Stand* conference. We stayed with Emmett's mom. One night we were sending balloons up to heaven, and Bostyn handed hers to me. It said something like this.

Dear Daddy Emmett,

We miss you every day and love you so much. Thank you for always watching over us. I know it was you that sent Scott into our lives. Thank you for being our angel and sending us one to be with us here on earth. He is so kind and good to us, and I am so glad you found him for our mom and for us. I know Heavenly Father let you pick him for me.

Scott is made from a different mold. He is so kind. He is so steady. One of the weekends after I introduced him to the kids, as he was driving away, Tytus started crying. I was taken by surprise.

I said, "Buddy, why are you crying?" He said, "Because I want Scott to come back." I said, "Oh man, me too, buddy. What do you like about him so much?" Tytus' response made me cry, "Mom, can't you see all the light angels that are with him?"

And that's what I feel when I am around him. Light. Peace. Love. I feel whole. This time it is a whole that I found first inside myself.

I didn't follow through with my vow. I didn't kiss my ten guys or go on dates for years, but I found my person. And the kids and I have never been this happy.

It's pretty easy to stop believing in love because love doesn't always last on all the paths that we walk, and those we love aren't always kind. But your ability to love never dies because we were created to love as Christ does.

A few hard days and then faith in the plan.

When God closes a door, He opens a window. He is so good. He has blessed me in ways I never knew were possible. I have seen many miracles in the midst of what I assumed was failure. I am so thankful for a Father who knows more than I do. I am humbled by His plan.

We are so blessed. I keep telling Scott one day we will write a book called *Patiently and Impatiently Waiting: A Divorced Widow and 39-Year-Old Single Guy's Journey to Love*. He doesn't think I am funny, but man, what a ride we have been on to find each other. I am just so thankful he had the determination to wait for me, because there has been nothing in my life that has been so sweet.

Life keeps moving forward and love is still possible. We are creatures worthy of giving and receiving love, no matter what our story.

Here's to new adventures and faith in a plan—God's plan. I trust Him and see His hand on all the broken roads that have led me here. A perfect mess that has been abundantly blessed.

CHAPTER TWENTY

The Strength of the Buffalo

IT HAS BEEN MORE THAN a decade since I started my journey of becoming a Buffalo. Let me explain:

Storms. We all face them sometimes. The hardest ones are the kind that come out of nowhere with dark heavy clouds that threaten our very existence. In the animal kingdom, no one is exempt from them either, but there is one animal who has it all figured out.

When storms come, what cows (and other roaming animals) do is very natural. Cows sense the storm coming and immediately start to run in the opposite direction. The only problem is they aren't very fast, so the storm catches up with them quickly.

Without knowing any better, the cows continue to try to outrun the storm, but instead of outrunning the storm they actually run right along with it. Thus, their frantic running away from the storm *maximizes* the amount of pain and time and frustration they experience in that storm!

A struggle that could have ended more quickly seems to carry on for a very long time, leaving the animal exhausted, defeated, and even permanently injured.

Buffalo, however, take a different approach to storms. Buffalo wait and watch as a storm approaches. They remain relatively calm and keep their eye on the raging clouds. When the weather is close, the buffalo turn toward—and charge directly into—the storm.

Instead of running away from the storm, they run directly at the storm—straight through it—thus minimizing the amount of pain, time, and frustration they experience from it.

It has been many years since our biggest storm. Sometimes I have been the cow, wandering aimlessly, trying to outrun and hoping to get ahead of the raging storm. Other times I have been the buffalo with my head down, charging it, ready to fight, ready to get through, ready to stand strong on the other side.

The hard stuff in life either breaks us and wears us out or gives us a strength we didn't know we were capable of. The pain we carry either works to hold us back or gives us a reason to keep pushing through.

We can learn a lot from the buffalo. Even in the times we can't see the storm coming, we can still decide in a moment if we will lean into the coming storm or if we will spend the rest of our lives trying to run from it. Either way there will be moments we'll have to face it, either head on, or as it knocks us over from behind.

So many have shared my buffalo stories with me. I have learned from stories of perseverance how to be better. I have gained insight from other's experiences on how I can strengthen myself.

I cannot think of the strength this girl, who started this journey all those years ago, has gained without picturing all of you who have supported me. You have seen the goodness in me I thought was lost when that gun fired. You have given me a space to own my story instead of running and hiding from it. And like the buffalo, you have helped me find the strength to hold my head high, grit my teeth, and keep stepping into the storms life has sent.

That day we said goodbye to a lot of things. One of those was our innocence. That has been a hard one to find again. But through the years of buffalo moments that have followed, we have gained way more than we lost.

I will never be the same innocent young mom who sat on that couch and had her heart ripped out of her chest. I know now just how cruel this world can be. But also, I will never forget that moment I stepped into my closet and prayed harder than I have ever prayed.

I will never forget the light that filled my heart and mind, promising me a brighter day. Promising me that I could learn how to truly forgive; promising me that someday I would be able to breathe again. That moment and that prayer gave me a glimmer of what could be. That prayer and that promise gave me the strength to walk forward—just like a mama buffalo—into the storm.

Just like you, this mama buffalo has seen other storms. Honestly, I know that life is always going to have storms that will show up when we least expect them.

Years after the murder trial ended, I watched Emmett's dad take on one last storm. He battled esophageal cancer. One day the storm got to be too much, and we had to say goodbye.

We spent an entire summer cleaning out his house. It felt like the twilight zone cleaning out the belongings of three people I had loved so much. Emmett, his step mom Danise (who had passed away right before Teage was born), and his dad Mike were the only people who had ever lived in that house. All of them were gone.

Each day I had piles of memories I didn't know how to get rid of, but I had nowhere for them to go. One day I found something beautiful. Emmett's dad, or Papi as he had asked all the kids to call him, had kept a notebook at the murder trial. Most of it was thoughts about different witnesses taking the stand. Scattered on each page were little thoughts about what he could see in me. He talked about the pain he could see in my eyes. He talked about how he wished he could take it from me. He wrote about how he came every day to be there for me.

To be honest, I didn't even see him there. I didn't see anyone but myself. I didn't take notes about wishing I could make things easier for him, because I was too wrapped up in my own storm. He literally walked in every day in pain, fighting cancer, and still took the time to see me. I didn't even realize his pain, until I held his hand in some of his final breaths. It hurts me still to think about all I could have been for him. I could have seen him, and all I saw was me.

Sometimes the storms are so dark, we feel alone even when we are surrounded by people. Papi chose to see me, even in his dark storm.

Some of my darkest storms have come watching my children fight their darkness.

Before, and especially during the big Covid-19 quarantine, I watched my daughter Bostyn fight her way through an eating disorder. Soon, there came a time when we knew she needed help beyond what we could give her.

For three months she lived in a facility where they kept her alive and gave her a place to heal and find herself. That pain as a mom was more than I thought I could take. I felt helpless the day I dropped her off and had to walk away. I have never cried so hard and pleaded so helplessly as I did that day.

Sometimes the hardest storms are the ones we watch others face when we can do nothing to take it away from them. The helpless storms are when we have to cheer from the sidelines to a buffalo that has given up.

There will be storms. Sometimes you will be looking in and sometimes you will be pleading to get out. I know those clouds are dark. I know the pain is real and the wounds run so deep, but don't you dare give up.

This storm will pass and the light on the other side will find you. One day it will all make sense, but for now, just keep putting your head down and getting through to the other side. I promise you will find the light again.

Don't spend too much time being lost wandering, afraid, and running from the storm. You were not created to cower—you were made for greatness. You've got this, brave buffalo.

CHAPTER TWENTY-ONE

Get to Work

ONE NIGHT I HAD THAT bad dream—the one with the crying baby and the slammed door and the gun. Only this time when I got to the part where the detectives came and told me about Emmett's murder, I was sitting across from myself. I was both characters.

In one moment I could feel all the pain from the past. Then the next moment I became the other person and I bore my soul to myself. I talked about angels and grace. I told myself about all the moments that I knew I wouldn't be alone. I pleaded with myself to fight and screamed all the reasons why I was going to have to be strong.

Then I became her again—the broken girl. Alone. Afraid. I looked around the room as it began to spin, the voices of my new reality swarming all around me. My eyes searched for something to look at. And then there I was … I looked into my own eyes staring across from me. I could feel myself pulling me to fight. I could feel the whirlwind of fear trying to bring me down. It was almost like a battle between darkness and light.

But then all the sudden, I was filled with this immeasurable amount of strength. In my head I heard my own voice calling my name and saying, "Ashlee. It will be hard, it will be dark, it will be humiliating, it will be lonely … and it will feel impossible. But you will stand."

All of a sudden, the noise became more quiet. The voices of the detectives still repeated the facts of that night, but the little broken girl who once sat alone on the couch was standing.

And you will too!!!

For the next few chapters, we are going to be going over some assignments to dig into your story, to open some opportunities for your own healing, and to help you assess some spots you could be stuck and some options beyond living life stuck!

If you enjoy these next few chapters, please visit my website and join me for one of my online courses. Every day I get to help people own their story, find their peace, and start writing a new story. I would love to go there with you too!

I first wrote this book many years ago from a different perspective and then felt I needed to start over and share so much more than the pain. I have found that my victimhood was a choice, and I have felt empowered realizing I was the one who could change the tone of this book, and ultimately the tone of my life.

You deserve this same freedom. I want you to walk away from reading this series with tools to help you become more than just a victim of your circumstances. I want you to become a conqueror.

CHAPTER TWENTY-TWO

Dear Trauma

HERE IS YOUR FIRST ASSIGNMENT: buy a journal.

I write a lot of letters in my journal. Most days I write to God—like a prayer on paper. And I love to pray and ask Him to write back. Some days I feel inspired to write a whole bunch of things to myself. Other days I feel impressed about one particular struggle or insight. Sometimes I write letters to the people who have hurt me. Some I have sent. Others I have burned.

So for your first assignment I want you to write a letter. Maybe you won't ever send it. Maybe the person you are writing it to has passed away. Or maybe, like me, your letter is going to be written to something. Figure out what you are going to write, find a quiet spot and let it all out.

Here is one of mine:

Dear TRAUMA,

You took something from me I can never get back. You made me believe that my life was not my own. You left me paralyzed in fear. I struggled to get back up, wondering if I was enough and wishing I could know why you chose me.

It seems you had a plan; I was your victim. You chose a side, and it wasn't mine. You didn't wait around to help me get back on my feet; you didn't ask if I was OK. You just made your mess and then left me to figure out the rest. I had to pick up the pieces alone.

You knew that moment would try to define me. You knew that fear would swarm the memories of the past. But even worse, you knew that it would try to hold me back in the future, making me unable to breathe.

I was broken; my tears were immeasurable. At times I felt alone, and despair was my constant companion. I searched for something to hold onto for hope, but you had taken all of that from me. You laughed at me as you walked away. That was the hardest sting: when I watched you not care.

You probably thought I would stay down forever—that a bird with a broken wing would never fly again. You probably hoped I would give up. You probably didn't even look back to make sure I was still down.

Turns out, even broken wings can mend. It turns out, I was a lot stronger than you thought. I bet you didn't know I was a fighter when you chose me as your victim. I bet you didn't realize that strength can grow from a tiny sprout of faith in God. I bet you didn't expect to ever hear from me again. I bet you thought that my life would now be yours. I bet you always thought I would forever be your puppet.

Well, today I stand to not only tell you, but to show you that you were wrong about me. You thought you chose a victim, but it turns out I am a survivor. Your puppet has cut the strings. I will no longer live in the shadow of your fear. I will no longer hate in the chains of your anger. I will be free. I will build from this ground that you threw me upon, and I will become stronger.

So maybe you saw my weaknesses as you tried to make me fall, but guess what: I saw yours too. Your weakness was thinking that you would ever bring me down without a fight. I am a warrior of my own life, and I fought against your evil plan.

I am a champion who sees through the fog and clings to the light. I found hope when you told me there was none, and I will live every day unbroken. You did not break me when you dropped me on my face—you taught me how to stand.

Sincerely,
Me

Each time you write, you are releasing emotions and letting out trapped pain. It might feel strange at first, but keep showing up with your journal and writing from your heart. You might not end up turning it all into a blog, like I did, but it can be healing for you as you look back on how far you have come and all the insight you have gained.

CHAPTER TWENTY-THREE

Look Up

AS A TRAUMA HEALING ASSIGNMENT on my blog, I asked my readers to write a story with themselves as the main character.

As you write, pay attention to the strengths your character has, and remember some of the moments your character has been brave and strong in ways you haven't even realized.

Will you write from a narrator's perspective? Will you speak from the character's point of view? What will your character be doing?

Here is mine. I hope if you have ever "stood alone at the edge of a cliff," you can deeply feel the truth and light that the girl in my story began to live. I know the truth will make a difference in your mission and help you find your purpose here on earth.

Look Up

She stood at the edge of the cliff, watching the rocks fall beneath her feet. It was hard to see what was on the other side through the fog. She looked behind her—all that was left of the trees were trunks still smoking and black. She looked down the canyon. Up and down, the water rushed through the gorge, the caps were white and she could feel the chaos that churned in their power—each rapid reminding her of the storm that raged inside.

At this point she had only two choices: jump and never have to feel *any of the pain ever again, letting the water take it all away, or turn around and try hard to find her way through the wreckage alone so she could get back to the place that took everything from her and pretend life was worth living.*

Time stopped as she stood at the greatest crossroad of her life. Looking down, nothing seemed promising; a fatal steep drop was the easy way out. Looking back provided a darkened broken picture of what once was. The view of the mess sent chills down her spine and a pit of fear sunk in her stomach.

She didn't want to die, but she could no longer live as if she were dead. Her eyes didn't know where to turn their gaze—every direction was a reminder of her worthlessness. She was not enough. Yes, this was all the evidence she needed—this moment made everything so clear. For the first time in her life, she had nowhere to turn, and worse, no one by her side.

Did anyone care that she was alone? Would anyone notice if she wasn't there? Her life—or her death—wouldn't affect anyone else, so what did it matter? She wanted to just jump and make it all go away.

Each thought and each glance brought about more and more fear. She was frozen, broken, and alone. It was her darkest hour. She thought about her life, each moment leading up to this day—all the broken promises and pain. She thought about her death and wondered if she had already been forgotten. She didn't know who to be angry with: herself, everyone else, or maybe God?

"Hey God ... are you out there?" She could hear her voice echo through the canyon walls. "Can you hear me? Can anyone hear me?" She looked behind her again. No one. She looked down the canyon right and left—nothing. She held her head down and stared at her bare feet.

"I am going to die here and no one will care. No one can even hear me." Her pleas began to grow louder, "I am going to die here ... please don't let me die alone. Please let me just have one do-over. I am so scared and alone and humiliated and so, so forgotten."

Soon the fog began to surround her. It was so thick even the canyon view began to grow black. She looked back to more darkness. At the edge of the canyon the world went black and she was surrounded by her fear of being alone. She stood in the darkness battling her demons.

Hours passed, each one bringing more and more panic and a greater and greater need to look down and check behind her. Total darkness, utter isolation. Her eyes began to scan the world for any glimmer of light—and that is when she realized she would have to look up.

As her eyes gazed toward heaven, she felt a peace unlike any she had ever known. For a few minutes time stood still, and she could finally see. Like a movie playing on a screen, she could see herself living a life—her life.

She saw a glimpse of light in her eyes, and beauty in her soul. A magnificent love surrounded her and for a split second she knew in her heart that God had a plan. In that moment she could see herself on the other side of the canyon. She was not only living—she was laughing and smiling, and she was standing tall.

But how could this be? A broken girl, with a broken soul. She could never be whole or loved. She could never be enough. Or could she? With nothing but a glimpse of a promise, she set out on her journey in the dark.

She decided she would move forward, even if she had to take just one step at a time. For the first time in her life, she would live each day with grace, knowing that she could not change the past, but she would have a future. She was still stuck in the fog at the edge of a deep canyon, but she was going to live.

And that is what she did. Some days she could barely see with so many tears in her eyes; some moments she couldn't breath with so much pain in her heart, but day-by-day she began to find herself.

You see, the angels couldn't just pick her up and set her down across the canyon. But they walked with her through darkness, they battled with her through the valleys and the streams. They showed her the pathways to take and the hurdles to cross, and eventually they helped her find how to become that girl—the one smiling and standing on the other side of the canyon.

She saw many miracles in those dark days, but the greatest gift she received was the rocky course—the bumps and the bruises—that taught her how to fight. It wasn't until she hit rock bottom that she realized she *was only halfway living when she was at the top.*

Strength came when she had to find out for herself just how strong she was. That fight is what showed her that she had worth—that she was enough for God. It wasn't an easy road, or a paved path, but she fought every step of the way. And as she looked toward heaven, she was reminded how—not why—her journey was different from the one she had planned, and she knew without a doubt that she was never alone.

He was there through that fire. He was standing with her by that raging water. He was catching the pebbles that crumbled under her feet. He felt every pain, He heard every fear, and He wiped every tear. He was always there, but the moment she could finally feel Him was when she decided not to look down, not to look back and wish for what was, but to LOOK UP.

Your assignment is to answer this question:

> *If you were the character, what would your story be? Write it down in your journal.*

CHAPTER TWENTY-FOUR

The Same Story, Different Ending

I REMEMBER BEING IN COLLEGE and reading about a study done by a psychologist with hundreds of sets of identical twins. He was most fascinated by a set of twin brothers. One had gone to medical school, had a family, and a beautiful wife. The other had been in and out of prison, on drugs, and held no job.

In separate interviews he asked them a series of questions. All of the questions were the same. The last was, "Why are you the way that you are?" The inmate bore his soul as he shared. He said, "You know, when I was a little boy, my mom used to beat me and lock me in the closet. I have never really told anyone this. I knew right then and there that I was not worth anything. I knew in those moments that I never would be."

Then it was the other brother's turn. When asked the same question, his answer was powerful. He said, "I have never really told anyone this, but when I was a little boy, my mom used to beat me and lock me in the closet. I knew right then and there that I was worth more than she was telling me I was. I knew in those moments that I was going to make something of myself because I deserved to be better than broken."

We are all going to be given the chance at one point in our lives to be better than broken. We are not made up of the lies others have told us. The secrets do not have to change who we will become. Everyone deserves a reason to stand greater than we were before.

Whatever your story may be, I know it has been hard. Don't let others make you believe that your hard experiences are evidence of everything you aren't worthy of. Decide now. Are you the brother who believed the lies or are you the brother who is going to keep fighting for the truth?

> *I want you to write your story. Maybe it isn't one that can be shared with anyone else, but it is one worth writing. Start from the beginning with honesty and an open heart.*
>
> *Get it all out. Every pain, every moment of trauma—how did it feel for you? What were the good times? What were the hard ones? What were the lessons? What were the failures? Hint: a lot of times the lessons come through the failures. But I don't want to give away all the truths you are going to find as you write.*

Maybe you will get done and feel impressed to send it to me to share on my blog. I would love that. Maybe you will get done and feel impressed to burn the hell out of the paper it is on. Roll with whatever comes and love the person feeling every emotion that you feel. No shame. No betrayal of your feelings. Just love, truth, and a hope that once it is out, you can not only embrace it but love every character you have played. It takes bravery, and it will be a lot of work, but it will be worth it.

> "Owning our story and loving ourselves through that process is the bravest thing we'll ever do"
>
> Brené Brown

CHAPTER TWENTY-FIVE

Evidence

SOME DAYS IT FEELS LIKE we are doomed to fail. We're constantly at battle with the powerful personal voices in our head—one reminding us of our worthlessness and one gently whispering truth.

The louder one most of the time seems to overpower the soft. The tenderness, we begin to perceive as weakness. So we walk around, sometimes for decades, believing we will fail.

We start to live as if those bold lies in our minds are really who we are. The soft voice that once told us our truths feels distant and far away. The carefree life of long ago fades. The child who once didn't care what anyone thought is replaced by a lonely soul, seeking for proof that someone cares.

Every day we search frantically for evidence of our worth, but most days we fail because our expectations of what "love" and "respect" and "success" should be are never met.

Even when we achieve a goal, we want more. Our desire for perfection in ourselves is projected onto everyone who crosses our path. Their mistakes become evidence of their worthlessness, their tenderness makes them seem weak. Even when someone comes and does everything right, we use it as evidence that they must be fake or too good to be true, or stupid for spending time with a person who is so fractured.

So we keep searching for evidence of our worth, all the while never finding it. But we want it. We want evidence that we are loveable just the way we are. Evidence that someone cares. Evidence of a higher power—an eternal love that we know we are promised, but can't seem to find.

We search for evidence of a world that will see us, a relationship that will cure our pain, a friend to coax us along and tell us the words that will help us to keep moving forward, a soul mate that we can live life for, someone who helps us remember who we are. Because we have seen all the evidence, there is no way we are going to possibly be able to find it on our own. Because it is our very significance that is in question.

We use "signs" as evidence that the planets are aligning despite our imperfections—instead of seeing something as a blessing or something we have obtained because of our goodness or hard word. We are a walking contradiction. We use other people's mean words as evidence that we shouldn't let anyone in. It becomes proof to justify our own cruelty to ourselves. We use another's hate as evidence that there is no one who we can trust. We don't see that we don't even trust the very voice that is inside us.

The voice grows louder, and soon it is all we can hear. Every word spoken around us and every action taken by another person feels like evidence of how stupid, fat, ugly, dumb, lazy, selfish, alone, and pathetic we really are, and we lash out with proof that we have been wronged—never taking accountability for our actions, words, or fears. We always blame another person when we don't feel like we're enough.

We try to hide all the things we have learned to hate about our perceived self, making us live a fake life—one where we can hardly remember our truths. We hope we can accomplish some of our goals before anyone figures out the "truth" of our worthlessness and realizes that we only achieved them by accident or mere coincidence.

We are too broken to let anyone in, but too prideful to admit we are hurting. We get into toxic relationships with someone else who feels insignificant. One becomes the narcissist whose coping is to make life about them, the other the magnet that attracts someone who lets them make the world about everything but themselves. The dance becomes one of pushing people away, the other pulling tight to keep them close.

A chase of cat and mouse, all the while neither one living their truths and being their true authentic self.

It becomes easier to just be alone, because at least all we have to battle are the voices. With no one close to us, we assume we won't have as many chances of hearing or seeing evidence of our worst fear that we already assume is true: that we are worthless.

We begin to hate other people for not showing us how to find what we thought they could—ourselves. We fight for more time, more affection, and more love, but we don't know how to give it.

We want someone to just love us the way we are, but we don't even know how to love the person we see staring back at us in the mirror. We blame others for their lack of love because we wished we could find it inside. We give them the job of fixing our fears without any way of ever accomplishing it.

We hear people talk of grace and wish it could apply to us too. But that voice chimes in and says, "Oh no, not you. Grace is only for those perfect people you see at church. His love is for people who have earned it. Jesus has given up on you. You have made too many mistakes. You have gone too far. I need you to remember: you are not enough."

So we hang our heads down and wait for the day we can become less broken and more perfect so God will remember us. And every time we feel forgotten by Him, we hold in our hands more evidence of our worthlessness.

Evidence. I want you to ask yourself this one question: *What am I still waiting for?*

Our search for evidence will drive us. It will send us down dark windy roads seeking proof and fearing truth. It drives us to sit in courtrooms for months to hear the truths we hope will heal our broken hearts. It drives marriages, divorces, affairs, and abuse. It drives anger and fear. It drives us crazy.

So if you are one of those souls like I have been many times, seeking for someone or something to come and complete you, I need you for this moment to *stop*.

That battle in your mind between dark and light and truth and lies that is causing chaos and contention and fear is a lot simpler than we think.

We all know it well. That little voice inside our head—sounds very similar to our own—that always brings up our insignificance. Anytime we mess up, or worse, anytime we are about to succeed, the voice starts on us about all the reasons why we will fail, even replaying over and over all the times we have. It wants us to believe we are too small and we should just give up.

Insignificant feelings, dark pain, thoughts that make us shrink, or puff up to think we are better. Anytime we feel pulled to show up as something we are not, tempted to hide, or become something different… these are the voices of the dude. The dude is loud, persistent, and doesn't sleep.

The dude says, "Remember that one time you messed up? Dude. You are such a loser. Don't even try. Don't show up, you aren't worthy. Nobody will ever love you."

And the list goes on. The dude has one purpose: to hold us stuck!

First of all … these thoughts are not truth. They are not light. They are the voices of our pain, fears, trauma, and of the dark.

As we begin to distinguish truth from dark, here are a few ideas to think about. When you get a thought, remember:

1. If it brings you light … it is truth

2. If it leaves you feeling small, overwhelmed, or fearful … it is not truth.

3. If you feel trapped, lost, or a pit in your stomach … it is dark.

4. If it helps you feel connection, hope, and peace … it is truth.

Truth does not come into our minds in the form of putting ourselves down. It comes in the form of helping us remember our worth, our gifts, and our purpose. It comes in the form of a still small voice that guides us toward our wholeness, His grace, and the best versions of ourselves.

Write them out sometime. The dude thoughts. Pray about them, ponder the purpose they have tried to serve for you. How have they tried to protect you? Are they serving you now? Are they bringing you closer to knowing your worth?

It is time to let them go. Replace them with thoughts or beliefs that help you feel light! Ask in your prayers to remember the truths you hold inside. Talk kindly to yourself. Listen to the voice that lifts you. Start changing the script in your head! It can be the start of changing your life!

There are no gray voices. They are either dark or light. The ones that cause chaos are not divine. The ones that bring peace and love and acceptance of yourself and other people, those are the still small voices from God and His angels.

Ask Him for the truth. The truth is this: You are enough. You are worthy. You are smart. You are real. You can succeed at love, at life, and happiness. And you are worthy of it. You are kind, and deep down you have a warrior spirit that wants to help you remember those truths you were born to live. The battle of your thoughts is just one of the many fights you are going to face, but you will not do it alone. God didn't forget you, and He never will. So start remembering Him.

Keep winning. Live life like it was all on purpose, because either way you are stuck here. You might as well make the most of every moment.

Let other people in. They need you, and quite frankly, you need them. It is OK to cry. It is OK to laugh, even if you know what it is like to lose. You deserve joy. It will come in little flickers of moments, sometimes through the pain. Choose the right, even when it feels impossible. Choose the light—He is the only way. He is the only One who can teach your heart to remember that *you are enough*.

And as far as dating advice (to all the young girls who message me about red flags): look for someone who is steady, who is kind even to a waitress at the cheapest restaurant in town. Find someone who can do hard things without complaining. Find someone who makes you feel like the best version of yourself, not because he wants you to change anything about who you are, but because he genuinely can just see you. Find someone who is a rock in what they believe. Find someone who lets you soar, be there for other people, and succeed, even in the small stuff.

But first, be someone who sees you. Be someone who cheers you on when you succeed, and when you fail. Find your worth all on your own! Don't ever try to become enough for someone else. Just be you and don't settle for anyone who doesn't like what they see. You deserve the world, and you will find it in someone else when you have found it first in yourself!

Now for your assignment to write in your journal:

What "evidence" has been holding you back? That dude in your head, what has it been saying?

What fears have you been cycling through that are no longer helping you?

What are you most afraid of?

If your fear came true, what would that mean about you?

Is worrying about it stopping it from happening? Or just stopping you from living?

What truths would you need to remember in your triggered moments that would help you overcome this fear?

What does your dude say? Write them all out. Go through them line by line and ask God if they are true. In your prayers watch for that feeling of light or confusion. Then ask what truths you can go to instead of the fears!

It is amazing as we release the emotions, beliefs, and things that hold us back, how much room we have inside of us to remember our truths, what makes us unique, and become connected to the person we were always meant to be.

CHAPTER TWENTY-SIX

A New Story

WHAT MAKES US ENOUGH? IS it the world? Is it people around us and their opinions of who we are? Or is it God? In my experience, becoming enough for ourselves cannot come from another person. Sure, another person can add to our happiness and help us in our search for worth, but the foundation of our beliefs of who we are have to come from within. And they have to be a direct view of God's love.

If we could only see ourselves how He sees us, we would know that we were created just the way we are—on purpose. We would see that He sent us here for a unique mission.

Once we connect ourselves to that mission and see our purpose here on earth and stay connected to God, we will become unstoppable. It won't matter how much "evidence" is sent our way to speak to our insecurities because we will be solid in truth.

Find that truth. It is there. God made you to be you. He believes in you, and He is never far away. Once you find Him and learn how much He believes in you, your mission will become clear.

I wish I were an expert on life. I wish I had all the answers to the why's in my path. I wish life didn't always have to feel so dang hard. But this I know: God is real. He is always near. Even in those moments when we feel alone, He hasn't forgotten us.

It isn't the "trials" in the courtroom of life that will help us feel complete. It isn't perfection, or even another person. The desire to feel whole will only come through faith in Jesus Christ and our Father. His grace isn't just for those final moments after death. His grace is for all the little moments in our lives.

Look around you; be His eyes. See the struggling mothers; see the lonely children. Be His hands. Serving others will bring peace to your battles. You are not alone. Each of us is fighting our own battle to remember His grace. The real battles are not against each other, but against our real enemy. The evil, the darkness, the dude in your head has a name. Satan. He has studied you just as Christ has, only his goal is unique. He wants to bring you down. Don't give up that fight.

This world is not divided by borders, religions, or skin colors. It is divided by hate, anger, jealousy, and fear. Look for the truth. Look for love. The truth of God's love can heal even the most broken soul.

If you feel like it is your soul that needs repairing, turn to God. Close your eyes and go back to that trauma. Smoke out the lies and replace them with truth.

The truth is this: you are enough. You always were and always will be. You are a unique son or daughter of God. You always were and you always will be. Many will come to deliver "evidence" opposing your truth. Stay connected to what is real. You do not deserve the pain that has lied to you for so long. It is time to say goodbye.

Goodbye to the trauma of the past. Goodbye to the story you have held onto that you felt you deserved to live. Let go of the story that tried to break you. Let go of the anger that has built walls around you. Let go of the victimhood that has suffocated you. Those chains don't have to be carried. He can break them.

If it has happened, then it was meant to be. You are not forever broken. You deserve to be happy through the highs and the lows. Happiness is a choice to believe that when God promised that He sent His Son to redeem us, He didn't make any mistakes. Not in the plan, or in any of the steps that got us right where we are. He didn't make any mistakes when He sent you on an imperfect path to perfectly bring you back to Him.

Someday when we look into His eyes face to face we will see why everything happened as it did. I can just picture Him saying, "Ashlee, I know that was hard. I know that you hurt, and you fell. I know that you cried. I saw you ache, and I felt the pain. I know that at times you doubted yourself and my plan.

"I know that you were scared and humiliated. I know that you were bumped and bruised, but, Ashlee, I know that you felt Me there. Because I saw that even when you had every excuse to give up on Me, you had faith. Every day you were given a reason to fall, but you kept going.

"Thank you for letting Me help you stand. It is in those crossroads, where many choose to fall that I saw you stand the tallest. Some days you were leaning on Me so hard; some days you tried to rely on your own strength a little too much, but you were always standing.

"Thank you for believing in Me, for seeing Me even when everything went dark, and finding yourself even when you were lost. Thank you for finding truth, for fighting for light. It is that fight that showed Me how much you wanted to be here. Your life was one of many conflicts and battles. That was always the plan. Those were sent to you to make sure you would fight for heaven. And just like so many before you, you showed Me that this is where you want to be. You chose heaven.

"Welcome home, Ashlee. We have been waiting for you."

I don't know what life will look like after we leave this earth, but I know heaven is real. I know we have a Father who is cheering us on. I know we have a Brother who came to earth to show us how to fight for truth. His life was one full of conflict and pain. He gave us the perfect example to follow of how to live a life full of grace—to forgive and love even the most broken souls.

Even His last words spoken before they hung him on the cross, "Father, forgive them for they know not what they do" can be an example of His love. We will have our own crosses to bear, but we can use our words for good.

Not all of us will leave this life being tortured by our enemies, but all of us will be given challenges that will test our faith—moments of overwhelming chaos and fear that will beckon us to hate.

Let us follow the example of our Brother Jesus Christ. Let us be forgiving and find truth even in the hardest of moments. These moments were perfectly designed to help us trust God, have faith in more than what we can see, and learn to stand.

Sometimes we have to stand by ourselves, but we are never alone. You are enough. You are enough for the one who created you, and you are enough for yourself. No matter where you have been and no matter where you are headed, God loves you. He didn't make any mistakes, even when He created you.

Maybe your life has been very different from the plan you had for yourself. Mine too. But I know with all my heart that I am right where I belong.

So maybe we can't prepare for life with our own plan. Maybe what we have to prepare for is to be flexible. Prepare for some valleys and mountains; prepare for imperfection. Prepare to be surprised. And remember: you are enough and more.

The real test isn't if we can stand alone. It is if we can remember to stand with Him.

To all the hurting friends who don't know where to turn, *look up*. Don't wait for the ending of a trial to live your life. Don't wait for perfection. It isn't real, but you are. Your light can change the world. Release yourself from those chains of victimhood. Don't wait for someone to come break the chains or cut the ropes. Let them go. It will feel strange because for most of us victimhood is all we know.

I can't promise you that you will always know what path you will have to walk, but I do promise that you will never walk it alone. He will send people who need you—sometimes in the most inconvenient of ways. He will send moments where you will not understand what it is you are supposed to learn. But when you are given the chance to look back without the chains of victimhood, you will see a survivor. You will see your strength.

You are a warrior. You survived something that would have broken anyone else. Your story isn't over. Keep going, and do it daringly.

CHAPTER TWENTY-SEVEN

The End

THIS IS NOT THE END. But it is the end of a trilogy I never knew I would write. It is the end of a wound I have held inside for so long. It is the end of my victimhood.

I am so thankful for the opportunities I have been given, for the support you each have offered, and for your prayers, your graciousness, and your friendship. I appreciate all the times you have shared my story, and I know it is healing more than just me. That is humbling and daunting and overwhelming some days. But even more, it is amazing to see God work in such a unique way with such a bullheaded stubborn girl such as me.

Many Halloweens back I picked out a costume for Kaleeya at the store. She hated it, but I didn't care. I told her to throw it in her closet, and when Halloween came, I made her put it on.

We got to the first door and the lady opened it up with a bowl full of candy in her hand. She bent down and said, "Oh my goodness, what are you supposed to be? Rainbow Dash?" Kaleeya snapped with her bullheaded stubborn girl attitude (not sure where she got that … wink wink), "Yeah, but just so you know, my mom picked out this outfit when I was at school."

So today I beg you to just enjoy the free treats that people are handing you. Don't worry so much about the "outfit" God threw you in without asking your opinion. I spent way too many years feeling ripped off and worried about the "outfit" that I almost missed all the little glimmers of light—the free candy, if you will—that He had sent my way.

After all the failed outfits (and last names—Facebook literally messaged me asking if everything was OK), after all the heartache, I am now a mother of seven … on purpose.

Scott and I have two little girls together. Kennedy Isla (May 2019) and Kylar June Boyson (December 2020). They are a bright light in our lives. They have brought a healing I never knew we needed. They are sunshine.

We have been reunited with Jordyn after years of not being able to see her, and that has been a great gift for my mama heart. I will always see that little girl as one of my own and am so proud of the woman she is growing up to be.

Go follow *The Moments We Stand* on Facebook and Instagram for the latest happenings. I try to post updates of our lives and share experiences and lessons along the way.

I close this book with one last plea: don't take a gun when words will do the job. Don't find love outside of the person you have promised to cherish. But even more, don't forget to enjoy every moment. Live life like it was all on purpose. Make a difference in the world around you. Be a light. Pray for your angels—they are always there. Pray for grace—you are worthy of it. And remember, you always were and always will be *enough*. Fight for that truth, embrace it, and never let it go. Believe in yourself. Believe in God's plan. You are going to make it.

Today is a gift, each lesson a step on your climb to the best version of who you were created to be. Make it count.

My story isn't over and neither is yours. This was just the beginning, a chapter of the story of your life. Forgive. Set the prisoner free. Not the ones behind bars, the ones you blame for your pain. Not the ones that hurt you, or weren't who they promised you they would be. Set free the prisoner in your heart. Release the chains that you carry, and start living free. The bonds you have held yourself captive in, it is time to let them go.

Inhale. Exhale. Do you feel that? That is what freedom feels like. Welcome to the next chapter. The main character of this story is you. You deserve the world.

You are worthy of this light. You broke the chains, and you are ready for what is next. Joy! Love! Laughter! You create. You bring light. You are significant. You are kind. You seek virtue. You are incredible. You are smart. You are powerful. You are worthy of grace. You are tender. You have feelings that you are safe to share. You know what you want and what you will allow around you. You are capable of all you are asked to accomplish. You are brilliant. You are funny. You find the positive in light, and create it. You are sunshine. You are beautifully unique. You are worthy of partnership and love. You are a child of God. You have a warrior spirit. You were created for greatness. You have a mission and a purpose on this earth. You have spiritual gifts that will help you on this path. You are honest. You have empathy for others. You have angels that will minister for you. You have the gift to find the good in yourself and in the world. You are loveable. You are a warrior. You are enough.

Believe these truths. Seek out others that help you feel light. Manifest positivity and set boundaries inside yourself so others value you too. Set goals physically, spiritually, intellectually and socially that help you get out of your comfort zone so you can always continue to become a better version of your best self. The balanced complete person you strive to be. Have grace for yourself when you feel stuck, and honest with your emotions. Be vulnerable so others know you are a safe place to bring their struggles. But most of all, be you. Because it looks so good on you.

A firefly would never know how bright it shines if it always lived in the light. If today feels like one of the dark days … it might just be one that is helping you remember to keep shining.

Your life has been full of heartache. You have survived the unthinkable. You have been a victim in too many stories to count. But please remember: your life has been full of little glimmers of light. Your story has been full of grace. You have also survived too many times to count.

Your life has been full of miracles. And the greatest one ... is you.

Now is your time. You will come out of this stronger. You will live many more moments. Some will be hard. Others will be full of joy. But in every moment, I know that as you march forth with strength and courage and a perfect view of your significance ... you will be standing.

It isn't just time to break the bonds, it is time to let them go.

> *"To forgive is to set a prisoner free and discover that the prisoner was you."*
>
> Lewis B. Smedes

ABOUT THE AUTHOR

ASHLEE BOYSON IS THE AUTHOR of the blog and book series *The Moments We Stand* where she shares her family's journey of healing after the infidelity and murder of her husband Emmett in 2011, just months after giving birth to their fifth baby.

Ashlee has shared Emmett's story on *Dateline, Dr. Phil, American Monster, Investigation Discovery, True Crime Daily*, and several other murder mystery documentaries.

Ashlee advocates for victims and families impacted by loss, grief, widowhood, murder, and infidelity. She founded *A Reason to Stand*—a nonprofit focused on healing and empowering survivors. She continues to help others through online courses, public speaking, personal coaching, and—of course—writing.

Ashlee remarried Scott Boyson, and together they have two babies, totaling seven kids, ages two to eighteen.

Ashlee believes that each day is a gift and feels grateful for the grace and hope she has found in her story.

For more information on Ashlee's work, including her inspiring books, speaking engagements, and incredible courses, visit themomentswestand.com.

Enjoy the book?

Please consider leaving
an honest review
on **AMAZON** or **GOODREADS**!

Thank you!